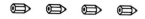

Your
First
Resume

Your
First
Resume

The Comprehensive Preparation Guide
For High School And College Students

By Ronald W. Fry

The Career Press
PO Box 34
Hawthorne, N.J. 07507
1-800-CAREER-1
(In N.J., 201-427-0229)

Copyright © 1988 by Ronald W. Fry

Your First Resume: The Comprehensive Preparation Guide For High School And College Students

ISBN 0-934829-25-X
$11.95 (postpaid)

This book may be ordered by mail or phone directly from the publisher. To order by mail, please include postpaid price, as noted above, for each book ordered. (New Jersey residents please add 6% sales tax.) Send to:

The Career Press Inc.
62 Beverly Rd., PO Box 34,
Hawthorne, NJ 07507

Or call **Toll-Free 1-800-CAREER-1 (N.J. residents — 201 427-0229)** to order using your VISA or Mastercard or for further information on all books available through The Career Press. An order form is included in the back of this book.

Table Of Contents

Another First In Your Life

There's a certain similarity about the "first times" in our lives—typically, they are challenging, exciting, demanding, rewarding, fulfilling, anxiety-producing. Think of the firsts in *your* life—the prom, a plane ride, trips away from parents and home, your freshman year at college. Firsts tend to be surrounded by a pulsating aura of exhilaration, anticipation and excitement. And, occasionally, that palpable sense of sweaty-palmed fear.

Preparing and successfully completing your first resume can bring about these same reactions. But forget the fears—it can be a pleasant experience...really! If you pay close attention to the steps outlined in this book and prepare your resume accordingly, you'll be on your way, happily blazing a successful career path. It's a trip worth taking, and Your First Resume will help you get there in great shape. Let me give you an idea of what you'll find in this book—the who, what, why, when and how of resumes.

WHO NEEDS A RESUME?

With the exception of the few of you lucky enough to be headed for a role in the family business, a well-constructed mini-biography of your experiences, skills and goals—your resume—is a fundamental ingredient in your initial job search. If you aren't convinced, simply ask yourself one question: Are you in transition? A "yes" means you need to prepare a resume.

If you are new to the game—about to enter the work force on any level—you are in effect beginning your journey from one mode of life to another. Your resume is the vehicle that will enable you to get there.

So if you are about to finish high school or college, receive a vocational educational certificate or re-enter the work force after any substantial interruption, get ready to write your first resume! Don't be afraid. You'll have plenty of company: It's estimated that 60% of the 5 million new job entrants this year will be called upon by someone, somewhere, to present one.

WHAT IS A RESUME?

Probably the best way to get a fix on what your resume *should* be is to become aware of the things it is *not*. Having reviewed thousands of resumes in my role as counselor and employer, I can tell you categorically that good resumes are *not* informal, lengthy, unfocused, lacking in pertinent detail, glib, aspirational, highly personal, chatty or overblown. They *are*, on the other hand, characterized by the same qualities that are the hallmarks of any good advertisement.

First, the best resumes are <u>targeted</u>—they state a concise objective of your goal that positions you on the road to a specific career. For example, one resume that recently crossed my desk presented the applicant's career objective as follows: "Space sales position using enlightened marketing techniques to generate above-quota sales results." This well-thought-through objective offers the reader (potential employer) the promised benefits of an applicant who obviously understands the main function of a sales job in the magazine publishing field.

As in any good ad, this promise of performance is <u>supported</u> by chapter and verse—reasons why this applicant is best suited for that particular job. These, of course, can include education, experience, transferrable skills, special skills and unique achievements.

I can't emphasize enough the need for <u>honesty</u> when you present the product! Supporting information must form a logical skills/experience safety net under the career tightrope you're preparing to walk. Applicants for sales positions who don't demonstrate a mastery of interpersonal communications skills, for example, would be well advised to re-think their career objectives.

And finally, as in any good advertisement, you have to <u>inform</u> the buyer where to find the merchandise (you). He or she may just be browsing, testing the waters to see how you'll hold up under in-depth inspection. But if you're serious about securing that all-important job interview, you'll make it easy for him or her to reach you. Name, address, phone number and *alternate* ways to reach you are essential bits of information the buyer must have if you hope to ever "close the sale" and get that job.

WHY DO I HAVE TO PREPARE ONE?

Why is a resume seemingly so essential? One reason is the amount of time employers have to spend fitting job openings and applicants together. The process is much like meeting a pretty girl or handsome guy at a party. The first meeting may be a mere glimpse across the room or a surprise encounter that passes almost before it begins. Quick! Do you seize the moment and try to start a conversation? If you do, and if you continue to find the other person interesting and desirable, you'll soon be spending more and more time together.

The employment process may progress similarly. It, too, can be remarkably brief—a quick glance, two-question meeting and thank you very much, the door's to your right. And just as everybody's after the prom queen and good-looking football hero, if you don't make a good first impression, you can be sure you'll be at the end of the line when it comes to allocating dances— if you're on it at all! Your resume is your calling card, and it better get someone's attention *fast*: The clutter of applicants for an interview means that you have only about 30 seconds to be noticed. Though that may sound unreasonable, unfair, unintelligent and arbitrary, it is *fact*.

In most career areas, the entry-level hiring process is not given that high a priority. A colleague reports that even prestigious Wall Street law firms have reduced their on-campus recruiting interviews to 20 minutes. While it hardly seems logical to limit so important a first meeting to little more than coffee-break time, the emphasis is clearly on first impressions. Your resume must catch their eye, strike a nerve, get the right chemistry going.

WHEN SHOULD I PREPARE MY RESUME?

Give yourself as much time as possible. There's an old saying— "Forewarned is forearmed." The job search process is not exactly like going off to war...but it *is* a highly-competitive process. My aim in this book is to give you the tools and hints you need to succeed in this competition. Getting your resume right and having it at the right time means you won't be fighting last-minute deadlines. Here is a handy guideline: Prepare your first resume draft just as you enter your senior year in high school or college, refine it at the mid-year break, then finalize it no later than Feb. 1st. This will give you ample time to plan, execute, edit and refine. It also maximizes the time you'll have to complete your all-important experience list. The job hunting season is an open one—your resume should be waiting to answer the very first nibble you get. Better to be ahead of the game than have to scramble when time begins to run short.

Don't plan your resume until your objectives have crystalized and you have some knowledge of the fundamentals of the job search process. Remember: You're not seeking a baby-sitting assignment or paper delivery route. It's a *real* job you're after, and you have to know where you're going in order to plan how to get there.

SO HOW DO I START?

A successful executive once confided to me that writing a simple business letter was a mind-numbing experience for him. He could communicate one-on-one, handle large-group presentations, use his ample business talents and skills to solve complex problems. Verbally, he was a whiz; on paper, he became a muddled, mindless mess.

After years of frustration, he discovered that his thoughts came much more easily at night. Away from the day-in, day-out distractions of his fast-paced business day, he was finally able to concentrate and lucidly translate his thoughts to paper.

We're not suggesting you lose sleep while preparing your resume. But you do have to make it a priority task, concentrate and, above all, follow the tried-and-true process I've outlined in the following chapters. Do that, and I guarantee you'll do it right—and with a lot less fuss (and more sleep) than my executive friend.

THREE THINGS YOU NEED TO KNOW RIGHT NOW

There's an old saying, probably one your parents love to throw at you: "Don't do as I do, do as I say." In preparing this work, I learned some new things about the job search process. Even after quite a few years of shepherding others and going through it (more than once!) myself. I think you'll be the beneficiaries.

Lesson #1: Plan

The most important thing I've learned is the amazing amount of structure and formalization that has creeped into the job search process in the last 10 years. Not that long ago, career planning was a hit or miss affair; it surely isn't one today. Even though I didn't do everything right when I started looking for *my* first job, I've learned how since then—and tested the techniques. Knowledge *is* power, and you can take advantage of my learning process.

Lesson #2: Do It Right!

..."or not at all," to accurately complete this sentence. In effect, a half-hearted attempt to follow all the critical steps covered in succeeding chapters is about the equivalent of doing nothing at all. So I urge you to recognize the importance of doing the job the right way. Like any work process, it will take hours, energy and commitment. Recognize the importance of what you have undertaken. Don't be distressed at the odds or the unknowns. Follow my lead and let me demystify the process for you.

Lesson #3: Some Experts Are Better Than Others

Some life subjects lend themselves more readily to the development of a cadre of experts than others. Career counseling, happily, is one of these. This book and the guidance it offers is the result of years of research, experimentation and field-testing. The data gathered has been subject to the feedback of numerous employers, recruiters, guidance personnel and human resources specialists. Obviously, advice can and will come to you from other quarters. Accept it, but with a modicum of skepticism. When all is said and done, think of Your First Resume as your primary source. Its job is to make *you* the expert.

STOP THE WORLD, I WANT TO GET ON!

That's my way of saying there's a lot to learn in the job search process and I think you are ready to get to it. Though I obviously can't stop the "spin" of the process, the following chapters will give you enough of the fundamentals to slow it down to manageable speed.

Before I give you a preview of what's ahead, be aware that there is an anatomy to the job market. As in any market, there is a dynamic give and take involved in its operation. Tough times mean a **buyer's market**—more applicants seeking fewer jobs. The classic symptoms are: harder to find openings, stricter salary negotiations, more and better developed skill requirements.

In a **seller's market**, the opposite is true. You can be choosier, command more money, speed up the process and usually negotiate from a position of strength—you'll have more than one offer to choose from.

Analyzing the state of the job market when you are looking, getting to know how it functions and learning about the key players are skills that will come in very handy for the long haul.

Now, some interesting statistics you will want to know about the market. It is very flexible and fluid:

- The average worker will change jobs three to five times in a lifetime
- 85% of all job opportunities are never announced publicly
- There are always new jobs—three to four million in the U.S. this year
- If you're between jobs, you'll need enough income to sustain yourself for about three months.

WHAT YOU'LL LEARN IN THIS BOOK

Here's a breakdown of the nine major areas you'll learn about as you read through this book. They're summarized here in the sequence in which you will find them. Since they are all interrelated, interdependent and sequential, don't skip ahead in your reading. If you just can't resist finding out how the mystery ends, I'll tell you now—it ends when you walk into your new office and start your first day on the job.

Chapter 1: An Attitude On Attitudes

I firmly believe in the power of positive thinking, which is why I stress self evaluation as a basic building block of success. It's *not* the easiest thing in the world to realistically assess yourself. The general rule is that you'll be successful at what you like best. But the work world is not that simple. There are many tasks you'll be called upon to perform in any job that aren't on anybody's wish list. Nevertheless, you'll need to master them.

This chapter will lead you through the steps to complete your own "Where Do I Fit" chart (and includes a sample list you can use as a guide). And remember what I said about a positive attitude: It's the great intangible in every job search. All other things being equal, the manner in which you relate to people—employers, interviewers, recruiters—will be the single, most important factor in separating you from the competition. The process sounds simple: First know yourself, then sell yourself. How you *do* each of those tasks is a bit more complicated.

Chapter 2: So You Want To Be In Pictures?

If you've been taking ballet lessons since the age of five, are musical, athletic and the best tap dancer in class, possess lots of energy and perhaps a touch of tunnel vision, you're probably already well on your way to a career as a professional dancer. No problem in getting *you* zeroed in on a particular industry or job function.

For most of you, the choice is not so clear-cut and obvious. You *can*, however, narrow the scope of this decision-making process by focusing on the career areas in which your skills (and the other things you learned about yourself in the previous chapter) indicate you will most likely succeed.

Chapter 2 will show you how. One surefire tip is to study the trade publications that cover the industry in which you're interested. You'll get an overview of the industry, a flavor of what it's like and how it sees itself.

By researching various industries, you'll also get a feel for their economic well-being. Why waste your brilliant computer programming skills on Silicon Valley if recession and the Japanese have hit this high-tech area?

Chapter 3: Corporate Culture—Finding That "Just-Right" Company

Birds of a feather *do* flock together. And different companies tend to attract, to a great extent, particular species. The overriding personality of each company—the kind of birds that predominate, especially at the top—is its **corporate culture**. Is it a "loose" atmosphere with jean-clad creatives running amok? Or a buttoned-down, blue-suited autocracy with timed coffee breaks? And how do you find out? A visit will give you some superficial information, but companies give off distinct signals of how they "think" in the way they treat their employees and the way they do business. And the word quickly gets out about those considered good or bad places to work...if you're prepared to listen.

The more you know about the company at which you wish to interview and how it describes various job functions, the better off you'll be. For those of you—and that *should* be all of you—who want to research a specific company and/or job description, this chapter will give you the necessary hints and resources, including a complete list of reference books that can be found in most local libraries.

Chapter 4: That's What Friends Are For

At a recent employment seminar, a college student asked me what I considered the most important activity in the job search process. While there really isn't one overwhelmingly-important aspect, I did have to acknowledge that **networking**—the process of making friends and utilizing them to develop referrals for either informational (information gathering) or traditional interviews—was the most difficult concept to grasp and apply, but potentially the key to any successful job search.

It's hard for many people to believe that "word of mouth" is the loudest trumpet proclaiming where and what the jobs are. But it is. By using friends (old and new), acquaintances and relatives, you'll soon build an ever-growing crowd of contacts who know you're looking, know you're worthwhile, will refer you to prospective employers...and expect you to return the favor somewhere along the line. Chapter 4 will show you how to implement this very important process and begin to develop your own lifelong network.

Chapter 5: A Place For Everything

You don't have to be a private detective to locate various agencies and programs that can serve as a link to job leads in your community—there's a whole host of resources out there, many of them free. This chapter lists those places you can go to for help.

Chapter 6: You're Ready To Write Your Resume

It's taken a lot of pages and preliminary steps to reach the point where you're actually ready to prepare your resume. But here you are! I'll discuss the various organizational formats that you can use (chronological, functional, combination), the information to include or leave out, and some basic rules to follow in preparing any resume, no matter how simple or complex.

Chapter 7: Try Before You Buy

This is a fun chapter, because it essentially puts you in the role of shopper—you'll have the opportunity to review 25 real-life resumes used by real people to secure their job interviews. Multiple examples of those utilizing the three basic formats are included, plus examples of specialty resumes, such as those for returnees to the workforce and returning servicemen. These samples cover a wide variety of industries and careers. Whether you aspire to be a clerk typist, financial analyst or (eventually) chairman of the board, you'll find a sample that will help you devise your own selling resume.

Chapter 8: Thanks And No Thanks

These are just two of the many different types of letters you'd better be prepared to write as you progress through your job search. Thank yous go out after informational and regular interviews, in acknowledgement of helpful advice and contacts. A good letter says many things about you—you're grateful, communicative, well mannered, serious about your job search and want to stay in touch.

"When you leave the pasture, don't forget to kiss the cows good-bye." When you're turning a job offer down, say thanks anyhow—you never know when you might want to reconnect with the company or the individual.

Both cover letters—in reply to an ad, cold calling, or as an inquiry—and follow-up letters—after an interview or in an attempt to find names of people to expand your own contact network—are covered in detail in this chapter. A number of sample are included.

Chapter 9: No More Sweaty Palms

Finally, all your hours of preparation have paid off—you're sitting opposite the operations supervisor of the ABC Widget Company. It's your first job interview! A computer programmer's slot is open, and you're being considered. Nervous? Who wouldn't be? Confident? Follow the tips in chapter 9 and you will be—it'll tell you how you can turn the interviewing process to your advantage, by knowing the types of questions usually asked (and your answers) and the types of questions you should be prepared to ask. You'll also find hints on dress, demeanor, posture, body language, the proper way to fill out a job application and how to handle psychological tests, which many large companies now utilize).

LET THE GAMES BEGIN

Exhilarating, challenging, rewarding—that's how we've described your first resume. This introduction serves only as a taste of what's to come. Taking the time to read through this book and completing the necessary exercises, lists and charts will give you the self-confidence you need to successfully maneuver through the job-search minefield. The only higher "high" is the sense of accomplishment you'll feel when you get the job that's right for you. It's a reward you will have earned. Enjoy it!

CHAPTER ONE ✏

An Attitude On Attitudes

This chapter, the most basic of all, is also the most important. Why? Because it establishes the foundation upon which the entire job search process—resumes, letters, interviews, etc.—must stand.

Who are you? No, don't just list what you've accomplished or describe yourself in "career-objective" terms. Who are you as a *person?* You must turn inward for the most important clues. Self evaluation is the technical term. If that sounds too serious, let's just call it "getting to know yourself." Your unique skills, values, likes, dislikes, strengths, weaknesses and "hidden skills" must all be identified, listed, analyzed and interpreted. When you're through with the series of exercises in this chapter, you will have some concept (perhaps for the first time) of the person lurking behind that face in the mirror. More importantly, you'll also have a much better idea of where you might fit in the broad puzzle called the job market.

IT SEEMS LIKE FOREVER

In the course of an average working lifetime—40 hours of labor a week—you will spend up to **60,000 hours** exercising a given set of skills. Making the most of that time—being productive and fulfilled—depends largely on how well you evaluate your dominant skills, especially right at the beginning. Correctly match your skills and interests to the right industry, company and job functions, and chances are your work life will be a successful and happy one. Should you be off the mark in the self-evaluation process, you will wind up in the wrong industry, at the wrong company and/or at the wrong job. The results are what you would expect from any mismatch—sub-par performance and frustration.

WHOSE LIFE IS IT ANYWAY?

Perhaps the simplest way to begin to describe yourself is to analyze what you think you already know about yourself and add some data on school subjects and extracurricular activities that may help indicate areas of strength and weakness. This exercise is geared to high school students; college or graduate students should adapt the questions to their own unique circumstances. Answer the following questions as best you can, writing in the space provided; there may be more than a single answer for each:

1. What are your best and strongest personality traits? (For example, are you honest, warm and friendly, inquisitive, cheerful, motivated, etc.?)

2. What are your best developed skills and abilities? (Are you a good cook, a tennis buff, musician, athlete, etc.?)

3. For each subject area listed below, check whether it's one in which you do best or worst, like best or least:

	DO BEST	LIKE BEST	DO WORST	LIKE LEAST
Art	❑	❑	❑	❑
Biology	❑	❑	❑	❑
Chemistry	❑	❑	❑	❑
Computers	❑	❑	❑	❑
English	❑	❑	❑	❑
Foreign Language	❑	❑	❑	❑
History	❑	❑	❑	❑

	DO BEST	LIKE BEST	DO WORST	LIKE LEAST
Math	☐	☐	☐	☐
Phys. Ed.	☐	☐	☐	☐
Physics	☐	☐	☐	☐
Psychology	☐	☐	☐	☐
Reading	☐	☐	☐	☐
Writing	☐	☐	☐	☐
Other subjects:				
_____	☐	☐	☐	☐
_____	☐	☐	☐	☐
_____	☐	☐	☐	☐

School Activities

4. In which extracurricular activities have you been involved during high school? Check all that apply in the first box below. Then rank your activities in order of their importance to you (with **1** being most important). Write the numbers in the second box.

ACTIVITY	INVOLVED IN	IMPORTANCE
Band	☐	☐
Baseball	☐	☐
Cable TV	☐	☐
Cheerleading	☐	☐
Cross Country	☐	☐
Danceline	☐	☐
Debate	☐	☐
Figure Skating	☐	☐
Football	☐	☐
Golf	☐	☐
Gymnastics	☐	☐
Hockey	☐	☐
Literary Magazine	☐	☐
Newspaper	☐	☐
Orchestra	☐	☐
Soccer	☐	☐
Speech/Declam	☐	☐

Student Government	☐	☐
Swimming	☐	☐
Tennis	☐	☐
Theater	☐	☐
Track	☐	☐
Wrestling	☐	☐
Yearbook	☐	☐

Other activities:

_____	☐	☐
_____	☐	☐
_____	☐	☐

Activities Outside School

5. List any volunteer work you do.

6. List any private lessons you take or have taken.

7. List any other clubs or organizations in which you are involved. Circle any that are particularly satisfying to you.

8. List any honors or awards you have received.

9. Are there any activities that you wish you had tried or would like to try? Please write them down.

10. Have you had any part-time or summer jobs that have made you curious to find out more about a particular field or profession? List those jobs.

Identifying Your Learning Style

The following series of questions will help you define how you learn best. This information is important additional data that will help you match the way you work, study and learn with particular jobs, careers, even companies. Check the answer in each set that seems closest to your preference. If you have no real preference in a particular set, leave the item blank.

11. While I am learning, I do best when I (or I prefer to):

A.　❑　Hear information
　　　❑　See information

B.　❑　Look at diagrams
　　　❑　Read descriptions in words

C.　❑　Look at maps
　　　❑　Read directions

D.　❑　Write notes
　　　❑　Concentrate on listening

E.   ❑ Answer questions with definite "rights" or "wrongs"
      ❑ Answer questions that can be debated

F.   ❑ Listen to music or television
      ❑ Have quiet

G.   ❑ Stretch out
      ❑ Sit in a chair

H.   ❑ Study a little each day
      ❑ Study a lot of material all at once

I.   ❑ Eat while I learn
      ❑ I don't need to eat while I learn

J.   ❑ Am near a window
      ❑ Am away from the window

K.   ❑ Have a lot of light (electric or sunlight)
      ❑ Have just enough so I can see

L.   ❑ Study alone
      ❑ Study with a friend
      ❑ Study in a group

M.   ❑ Have someone available for questions or help
      ❑ Study alone, but seek out help if needed

N.   ❑ Study in the morning
      ❑ Study in the evening
      ❑ Study in the afternoon

O.   ❑ Study under pressure
      ❑ Have ample time to study

P.   ❑ Read a lot
      ❑ Read only what is required for classes

Q.   ❑ Participate in doing something
      ❑ Be a spectator

12. How long can you concentrate well without a break?

    ❑ Less than 15 minutes
    ❑ 15-30 minutes
    ❑ 30 minutes-1 hour
    ❑ 1-2 hours
    ❑ More than 2 hours

13. How often do you feel bored in school?

       ❑ Never
       ❑ Infrequently
       ❑ Once a week
       ❑ At least once every day
       ❑ Most of every day
       ❑ All the time
       ❑ In certain classes (please list below)

14. Can you explain why you're bored at particular times or in certain classes?

15. What do you think you will need most in a company/job situation to be a successful learner? In other words, what environment best suits your learning and working styles? Summarize the factors from this list that seem the most important. (And when you visit companies, refer back to this list to determine if they offer the kind of environment you feel you need.)

16. What level of work challenge do you want for yourself? Think about not only the *quality* of your job and company environment, but also about how much *stress and pressure* you think you can handle and the *amount of time you want to pursue other interests and activities* outside of your first job. Check one of the choices below:

       ❑ The highest possible challenge
       ❑ A very strong challenge
       ❑ A good job, but one that allows me to pursue other things
       ❑ A good job with a relaxed atmosphere

17. How far do you want to go in your career? Check one:

❑ To the top—highest income, highest prestige (remember: often the highest stress and effort).
❑ Do it well...make a good living, be successful and work hard!
❑ Be good at what I do, but have time and energy for other things.
❑ Make a living and enjoy life in other ways.

(The previous series of exercises was adapted from the "Who Am I" chapter of College Comes Sooner Than You Think!, also available from The Career Press.)

THE GOOD NEWS

If you're six foot ten and adept at athletics, your skills will undoubtedly propel you to a career in professional sports—basketball stars, for the most part, are born, not made. In a word, you're a natural.

If you don't happen to fit this description but think anyone who does is simply lucky, you're right. But take heart—all of you have innate skills that will also tilt you onto particular career paths for which you're uniquely qualified. Think of the process of identifying these in terms of a funnel—broad at the top, narrowing as you get to the bottom. We want you to place all your skills in this funnel. Propelled by the force of so many items entering at the top, this flow of skills will gain momentum as it is forced through the narrowing tube until it bursts from the bottom. Along the way, some skills will be discarded, but the residue that remains—the pure nectar that filters through to the bottom—is the essential "you." To continue and refine the process begun in the previous section, you'll need a funnel (we'll provide it) and the raw ingredients—your skills (we'll give you a list of the most common from which to choose).

UNDERSTANDING THE INGREDIENTS

There is considerable misunderstanding about what constitutes a bona fide skill. Typing is a skill that can be readily understood and applied. But do you think of your abilities to store information, be a good listener or relate well to people as skills? They are and very important ones at that. Think of your skills as they fall into three major areas—person-to-person, informational and manual. This will help you further identify those skills you'll want to place in the top of the funnel as you proceed to determine your "Where Do I Fit?" profile.

A Smile For Everyone

This category includes those skills and abilities that enable you to comfortably and effectively interact with other people. They depend essentially on **action and reaction** and your ability to instinctively "read" and measure another's reaction to your action (or non-action). Simply put, they are "people skills."

Just The Facts, Ma'am

Computer printouts, accounting ledgers, inventory statistics—look at the desk of a data-oriented person and that's what you'll find. What I've termed informational skills are manifested in the ability to interact with things that, on the surface at least, can't react to you as people do. But analyzing, observing, evaluating and rearranging them soon gives them a life of their own—raw data becomes sales forecasts, quality control reports, profit and loss statements. The data may not be "alive," but it certainly has its own story to tell.

A Hands-On Kind of Guy Or Gal

We all know this type of person—he or she is "good with his or her hands." In this skill area, manual (and sometimes physical) dexterity and brute strength are at a premium—this is the person who can fix anything, assemble your kid brother's bike in forty two seconds and build a tree house that belongs in *Architectural Digest*.

TIME TO MAKE A CHOICE

Now that you understand the ingredients, it's time to begin assembling material for the funnel. This is the "Where Do I Fit?" part of the process. Chances are you'll find yourself favoring one of the three basic skill areas outlined above. But it's not necessary to limit yourself. If you find you have sufficient skills in more than one broad category, then work through the "Where Do I Fit?" exercise in as many as you can.

We've set up three simple tables for you to follow, one for each of the three primary skills categories, and a fill-in-the-blanks page you can use as your own worksheet. In each chart, we've catalogued basic skills by type, linked them to a work- or job-related characteristic, and then, finally, to sample (though by no means all) career areas.

WHERE DO I FIT? CHART—PEOPLE-ORIENTED

SKILL	WORK CHARACTERISTIC	CAREER AREA
Take instruction	Pay attention, carry out orders	Executive secretary
Serving	Execute wishes of others	Public relations, Nursing
Sensing, feeling	Able to "read" others' feelings	Telemarketing, Sales of any kind
Communicating	Give and take of information	Creative writing
Persuading	Generate action in others	Advertising, Sales
Performing, amusing	Work before a group	Law, Acting
Managing	Behave in a way that achieves an objective	Public affairs, Strategic planning
Negotiating	Give and take to achieve compromise	Politics, Sales, Psychiatry, Social work
Leading	Motivate by example	Corporate executive
Treating	Improve a condition	Counseling, Medicine
Advising	Give expert advice	Research
Training	Impart new information, ideas, procedures	Drama coach

WHERE DO I FIT? CHART—INFORMATION ORIENTED

SKILL	WORK CHARACTERISTIC	CAREER AREA
Observing	Good student of behavior	Accounting
Comparing	Identify similarities, dissimilarities	Quality control inspector
Copying, Storing language	Good memory skills	Foreign translator
Computing	Mathematical dexterity	Banking, Finance, Wall Street
Researching	Persistence	Scientist, Chemist, Engineer
Analyzing	See the whole and its parts	Movie or Book critic
Organizing	Adept at structure	Administrator
Evaluating	Good judgement	Vocational guidance
Visualizing	Symbolic perception	Interior design, Architecture
Improving, Adapting	Updating	Editing, Journalism
Creating	Turning data into something new	Securities analyst
Designing	Mold, re-shape	Packaging coordinator
Planning, Developing	Priority and sequencing skills	Systems engineer
Expediting	Speed	Office manager
Achieving	Reach or surpass goals	Athletic coach

WHERE DO I FIT? CHART—MANUALLY-ORIENTED

SKILL	WORK CHARACTERISTIC	CAREER AREA
Handling	Use of hands/body	Construction
Physical strength	Athletic coordination	Machinist, Metal worker
Earth and Nature	Making nature work for you	Landscaping
Feeding	Machine literate	Assembly line worker
Monitoring	Service machinery	Mechanic
Mechanical	Manual dexterity	Carpenter, Painter, Book binder
Vehicle skills	Regulating, controlling	Airline pilot
Precision	Work within set limits	Surgeon, Diamond cutter
Assembling	Organizing	Plumber, Electrician
Repairing	Understand how things operate	TV repairman

WHERE DO I FIT? CHART—FILL-IN-THE-BLANKS

SKILL	WORK CHARACTERISTIC	CAREER AREA

WHAT YOU SEE IS WHAT YOU GET—OR IS IT?

I wish I could tell you that's all there is to the self-evaluation process. In reality, there is a good deal more, though if you've completed the "Where Do I Fit" charts, you're already well on your way. But before we cry *"finis!,"* we need to complete one more step—identifying your **hidden skill**, the primary motivator that affects your overall intellectual, sensory or motor skill areas; in other words, what "turns you on?" There are only five such factors: Celebrity, Money, Power, Affiliation and Fulfillment. Discovering which of them is *your* primary motivator will help you to go beyond the obvious in choosing a career.

Celebrity

The strong desire for **fame** is a curious phenomenon that seems to distinguish Americans from most of the rest of world. Perhaps it is a natural corollary to our highly-developed communications apparatus; TV, radio and the press seem to make fame—even the instant, fleeting kind—so very desirable. Hollywood, a purely American invention, has made the concepts of stardom and "super"-stardom something to which to aspire.

Do *you* want to be a star? If so, you must choose those career paths that will give you the opportunity to achieve the celebrity you desire. But don't think of such careers in purely "artsy" terms like actor, rock star or anchor for the "Sunday News"—the activist corporate leader eager to cultivate an image as a leader and "doer" may be driven by the same lust for fame. The engineer who yearns to become the commercial spokesman for the new line of '89 automobiles has more than car sales on his or her mind!

Money

The desire for barrels of **money** is probably the easiest motivator to understand and the simplest to link to a variety of career paths. If your personal creed can be summarized as "I want, therefore I am," you probably fall into this category. So be prepared to abandon hobbies that can't be translated into dollars and look to investment banking, Wall Street, your own business, etc. in your search for the golden goddess. Make sure you know when and where the big payoffs are—they are usually short-term, high-risk, high-reward undertakings. Safe, secure jobs don't qualify. Make sure you are quick, flexible, risk-oriented, think in the first person, see yourself at the center of things and are able (and like) to see the Big Picture.

Power

A difficult motivator to assess because it comes with so much negative baggage. After all, "power corrupts," doesn't it? The flip side, of course, is "the power of positive thinking" or "the power of government to correct social ills."

If the **power** button is one which you must push, choose an area in which you will be quickly able to assume power and then exercise it. Again, this doesn't necessarily mean terrorizing the corporate boardroom or leading the arms talks in Geneva. An office manager in charge of a large clerical staff has power; so does a journalist (look at what Woodward and Bernstein managed to accomplish!). Choose a career that gives you control over people, issues and/or attitudes.

Fulfillment

If you believe that "virtue is its own reward," **fulfillment** is a prime characteristic on your hidden agenda. Choose one of the more altruistic career areas, one that allows you to do more for others than for yourself—work for a charity, become a legal aid lawyer, join a religious order. Or consider a creative career—while they may well become rich and famous, the primary motivator of many writers, artists, sculptors, etc. is to express their innermost thoughts and transform their audiences in the process.

Affiliation

While many companies will claim to be "like a family," few, if any, really are. But to the person motivated by **affiliation**, finding or creating the right work environment is critical—more important than money, power or fame. (It's their way of being fulfilled.) If you fall into this category, know what your potential employer stands for and be sure you're comfortable with it.

And be sure you'll be with people you'll like, those who share a similar outlook on life and work. If you love the outdoors, stay away from office jobs! If strict rules make you uncomfortable, consider a creative career in advertising, where jeans and sneakers and a modicum of craziness are *de regeur*. If you like wearing dark suits and white shirts—and being surrounded by similarly-attired co-workers in a stricter corporate environment—call IBM.

THE VALUE OF A SECOND OPINION

There is a familiar misconception about the self-evaluation process that gets in the way of many new job applicants—the belief that it is a process which must be accomplished in isolation. Nothing could be further from the truth. Just because the family doctor tells you you need an operation doesn't mean you run right off to the hospital. Prudence dictates that you check out the opinion with another physician. Getting such a "second opinion"—someone else's, not just your own—is a valuable practice throughout the job search process, as well. So after you've completed the various exercises in this chapter, review them with a friend, relative or parent. These second opinions may reveal some aspects of your self description on which you and the rest of the world differ. If so, discuss them, learn from them and, if necessary, change some conclusions. Should everyone concur with your self evaluation, you will be reassured that your choices are on target.

BE TRUE TO YOURSELF

Though there are certain mechanical guidelines you must follow to narrow down your career options, the system should (and does) have its human side, too. Attention to these intangibles—your innate system of values—is just as important as all the previous skill exercises.

You've already seen how skills analysis, the role of "hidden motivators" and the opinions of third parties interact to help you match yourself to a specific career; now you must ask yourself, "What can I live with?" All careers (and all jobs) exist in an environment that is the product of the combined values of the people that inhabit it. Though your skills profile may match up perfectly with the work characteristics required by a specific job, you will find yourself struggling (with yourself) if your values are at odds with those of the company. To guard against such an **"emotional" mismatch,** use the exercise in the next section to distinguish those overriding values that are most and least important to you.

A MATTER OF VALUES

VALUE	DEFINITION
Achievement	To bring any task to a successful conclusion
Aesthetic	Appreciation of beauty
Altruism	Selflessness
Autonomy	Self-independence, especially morally
Creative	Developing new, innovative ideas
Emotional well-being	Freedom from anxieties
Health	The general condition of body well-being
Honesty	Fairness, integrity, upright character
Justice	Impartiality; fairness
Knowledge	Recognizing the truth in people, situations, principles
Love	Warm attachment or devotion
Loyalty	Allegiance
Morality	Devotion to maintaining ethical standards
Physical appearance	Concern for one's body
Pleasure	Inner satisfaction
Power	Control, authority or influence over others
Recognition	Receiving deserved appreciation
Religion	Practice and belief in a supreme being
Skill	Abilities that can be used to execute an objective
Wealth	Abundance of possessions
Wisdom	Good sense, judgement

Which of these values are most important to you? Why?

Which are least important? Why?

Ask your parent(s) to identify their top three and bottom three values:

Describe a key value you feel you've gotten from your parent(s) and how this has occurred:

Discuss this exercise with your parent(s). Did you learn anything about themselves or yourself?

APPLYING WHAT YOU'VE LEARNED

Now that you've completed this seemingly-endless series of exercises, sit back, put your feet up on the desk and be proud—you've accomplished a good deal. You've answered a series of very important questions: What can I do? What do I like to do? What drives me? How do others see me? What are my values? You have begun to get some insight into the product you're preparing to market—yourself—and it's not a bad picture, is it?

At this juncture, adopt a seller's attitude. That is, *you* choose the exact career path you want to pursue, rather than seeing "what's out there" and applying haphazardly for anything and everything. In some cases the direction will be obvious—seemingly made for each other, you and your career will find one another. In others, you will need to set you targets—define those career areas that seem to be your most likely areas of success based on the exercises you've just completed.

Once you have decided on your list, you're ready to enter the research portion of the job search process—chapter 2 spells out how you can target and identify those industries in which your skills will be needed and those job descriptions for which you wil be particularly suited.

CHAPTER TWO ✏

So You Want To Be In Pictures?

As you move along the job search path, one fact will quickly become crystal clear—it is primarily a process of **elimination**: Your task is to consider and research as many options as possible, then—for good reasons—*eliminate* as many as possible, attempting to continually narrow your focus.

This chapter will help you begin this elimination process from the top—outlining the general criteria you can use to assess the current state and potential for growth of industries or professions you may wish to consider. You don't have to be bereft of any concept of a potential career to benefit from this chapter. Even if you think you know exactly what you want to do, researching the industry or profession you are considering will, at the very least, affirm your choice. Just as importantly, such general research will point out negative factors you must consider before you finalize that choice. Or even force you to completely reassess it. Better to find out now than on the job!

What you will be seeking in this process is a broad understanding of the winners and losers in the economic scene and why some industries and professions offer better long-term opportunities than others.

A good deal of background reading is required to accomplish this task. Begin familiarizing yourself with the bellwether business periodicals—*Business Week, Forbes, Fortune, Dun's Business Month, Inc.,* etc.—and reading the business section of your local newspaper. A periodic skimming of the *Wall Street Journal* would also be in order.

All of the resources mentioned throughout this chapter are the same primary tools you will utilize to discover information about specific companies and narrow your search even further.

GENERAL ECONOMIC TRENDS

The fundamental profile of the U.S. economy is changing—its historical emphasis on "making things" is waning, its long-term manufacturing economy shifting to a so-called **service economy.** Industries that are marketing- or sales-driven or concentrate on finance, promotion or the dissemination of information are those targeted for increased growth. Old-line industries like steel are expected to continue their downturn.

SHIFTS IN POPULATION CENTERS

Even a quick look at recent census data will reveal that a career in healthcare, especially for the elderly, is far more promising than one designing children's clothing. Why? Because America is aging—by the year 2030, senior citizens will represent 25% of the population, nearly double the current figure (13%). Those industries targeted to provide for the needs of the elderly will certainly benefit. Similarly, the end of the baby boom signals dimmer prospects for once-flourishing industries focused on children's products.

CHANGING LIFESTYLES

In the last two decades, our society has become more indulgent, with more free time and more money to spend on what used to be considered luxuries. As a result, a significant portion of our service economy is now dedicated to fulfilling those needs, whatever they are. Just consider, for example, the relatively new phenomenon of regularly eating out and the explosive growth of the fast food/restaurant business. As the role of the nuclear family has diminished, so have traditional family activities. Family dinners cooked by Mom are out—McDonalds is in.

Travel is another industry on a seemingly endless, upwardly-spiraling growth curve. Cheaper fares brought on by airline deregulation and the eternally romantic lure of far-off lands—of which we are daily reminded by satellite—indicate no end to our lust for travel.

Other service industries pegged to such lifestyle changes will experience similarly explosive growth.

OFFSHORE COMPETITION

Television sets, automobiles, steel, semi-conductors—all products or industries begun and developed in the United States. But if you buy such products today, it's likely you'll find a Made in Japan or Hong Kong or Taiwan label on them. The ability of foreign competitors to undercut our previously-preeminent leadership in manufacturing via cheap labor and government subsidies has seriously hurt, even devastated, numerous "American" industries. The result has been layoffs, restructuring, plant closings. If one of the industries on your list is labor-intensive and prey to foreign competition, think twice! Barring restrictive trade barriers or a trade war that nobody can win, there doesn't seem to be any hope that America can recapture its market leadership in many of these areas.

VARIATIONS IN THE LEVEL OF UNEMPLOYMENT

Current unemployment figures, depending on how you look at them, are encouraging or discouraging. Unemployment currently stands at 6%, as low as it's been for many years. But don't be mislead by such *national* figures—you need to look at the rate in *your own state or region.* Hard times in the oil industry, for example, have dampened the previously booming Texas economy. But if you're ready to work in New England, employers will be lining up to talk to you. If the industry group in which you're interested is concentrated in an already economically-depressed area, a downturn in a single industry may seriously effect all employers in the region.

And, of course, remember at what cost such low national employment has been achieved—monumental deficits that are already affecting our economy and may well lead to recession, even depression. Look for industries that are at least somewhat "recession-proof." (Few if any industries are *depression-*proof.)

CYCLICAL NATURE OF CERTAIN BUSINESSES

Some industries have a long history of upturns and downturns—booming for a while, then careening to the bottom. One example is textile production, bedeviled by a surplus of now-affordable machinery that can quickly flood the market with goods and the fickle nature of the fashion business. When the designers don't correctly perceive the pulse of the public, retail sales plummet, which reduces the amount of fabric purchased. Few can predict which way the pendulum will swing in any such industry, so be wary. It's a here today, gone tomorrow phenomenon.

GROWTH INDUSTRIES

Each year the wise men who report and comment on the world of business publish their lists of growth industries, those areas that, based on a number of economic and marketing indicators, are presumed to have the best potential. Electronics, computers, finance and healthcare seem to be on everyone's current list. I suggest you try to become your own "crystal baller."

Focus on the demand side of the supply-demand equation: If your common sense tells you the products of a particular industry will surely be in demand, you've identified a growth industry.

GETTING STARTED

Now that you know something about targeting industry winners and losers, it's time to put your expertise to work. Let's assume for a moment that you've assembled a list of ten industry areas you want to investigate: aerospace, data processing, toys and adult games, restaurants/food service, plastics manufacture, travel, airlines, exhibition sports, fishing/canning. (Quite an eclectic series, but ignore that.)

It's time to become acquainted with a key reference resource—the various volumes of *SRDS* (Standard Rate And Data Service), all of which are available in most libraries. The volume in which you're interested is Business Publications, which lists, by industry, the thousands of business (or trade) magazines published. You'll find the following listing of major trade publications under "Restaurant/Food Service," for example: *Bill Of Fare, Catering Today, Chef Institutional, Cooking for Profit, Food Management, Institutional Distribution, Restaurant News, Restaurant Business, Restaurant Hospitality, Restaurants & Institutions*. You'll find similar listings for all the other industries/professions you've targeted.

DIVIDENDS FROM THE BUSINESS PRESS

These trade publications are prime sources of information. Start reading them (many major ones are collected in metropolitan public libraries) and write for recent issues of the major ones in the field in which you're most interested. Making such reading a weekly practice will accomplish a number of important goals. You'll begin to absorb:

- General information on the industry as a whole
- Specific information on major companies in the field
- Trends, new products and the general outlook for specific product categories
- Major players in the industry—both companies and individuals
- Industry/professional jargon

In addition, published interviews with leading practitioners in the field will give you insight on how they approach their specific jobs. You can even consider calling these interviewees or the practitioners who write many of the industry articles. It's a good entree!

HINT: Look for news about recent or forthcoming mergers and acquisitions. Such movement often leads to shifts in personnel needs—while some pros may hit the streets as "carbon copy" positions are eliminated, entry-level people may be walking in the front door.

You'll also be able to flush out speciality publications devoted to careers or professions that cross industry lines—law, insurance, computers, advertising, etc. They're all listed in *SRDS*.

BY THE NUMBERS

"Bottom line" may be an overworked expression, but don't underestimate its real impact. Profit, after all, is the primary motive of the business world; sooner or later, the strength or weakness of a company (and industry) become apparent...on the bottom line. You can get a semblance of the strength of an industry by looking at the financial results of any of its leading companies. All publicly-held corporations are required by law to issue annual reports, which include detailed financial data. Call the company's headquarters and ask them to send you a free copy. Many major metropolitan libraries maintain collections of annual reports from major corporations.

REQUIRED READING

For more general research , you might want to start with How To Find Information About Companies (Washington Researchers, 1985), the Encyclopedia of Business Information Sources (Gale Research, Book Tower, Detroit, MI 48226) and/or the Guide to American Directories (B. Klein Publications, P.O. Box 8503, Coral Springs, FL 33065), which lists directories for over 3,000 fields.

Here's a primary list of research sources, most of which should be available in any library. These references will also be essential to garner more specific information on companies you've targeted:

• Dun and Bradstreet's family of corporate reference resources: the Million Dollar Directory (160,000 companies with a net worth of more than $500,000), Top 50,000 Companies (those with a minimum net worth of just under $2 million) and Business Rankings (details on the top 7,500 firms). Another volume—Reference Book of Corporate Managements/America's Corporate Leaders—provides detailed biographical data on the principal officers and directors of some 12,000-odd corporations. Who says you can't find out about the quirks and hobbies of the guy who's interviewing you? All of these volumes are available in most libraries or from Dun's Marketing Services (3 Century Drive, Parsippany, NJ 07054).

• Moody's Industrial Manual (Available from Moody's Investors Service, Inc., 99 Church St., New York, NY 10017)

• Standard and Poor's Register of Corporations, Directors and Executives includes corporate listings for over 45,000 firms and 72,000 biographical listings (Available from Standard and Poor's, 25 Broadway, New York, NY 10004.)

• Thomas' Register of American Manufacturing (Thomas Publishing Company, 1 Penn Plaza, New York, NY 10001.)

• Ward's Business Directory, a three-volume reference work that includes listings of nearly 100,000 companies, the majority of them privately-held, and details that are usually most difficult to acquire about such firms (number of employees, annual sales, etc.). Published by Information Access Company.

• The Standard Directory of Advertisers (also known, because of its bright red cover, as the Advertiser Red Book) lists more than 17,000 companies who commit some portion of their budgets to advertising and promotion. It is available in two editions—classified and geographical. Major product lines and the agencies to whom they are assigned are listed, as well as the names and job functions of key marketing personnel at both the listed companies and their agencies.

• **The Fortune 500** is an annual compilation by *Fortune* magazine of the top U.S. businesses, ranked by sales. It is particularly important later in your search, when you're targeting specific companies, as it will enable you to analyze not only where a particular company ranks in the overall U.S. economy, but also which are falling, which on the rise, and how companies measure up against others in their field.

One last note on potential sources of leads. The Oxbridge Directory of Newsletters (available from Oxbridge Communications, 183 Madison Ave., Suite 1108, New York, NY 10016) lists thousands of newsletters in a plethora of industries and might well give you some ideas and names. And the Professional Exhibits Directory (Gale Research Co.) lists more than 2,000 trade shows and conventions. Why not consider attending some to learn more about the companies and products out there?

Primary sources which should be utilized from now on to complete your research are The *Wall Street Journal, Barron's, Dun's Business Month, Business Week, Forbes, Fortune* and *Inc.* Naturally, the trade magazines which you've been studying (and to which you've already subscribed) offer a steady stream of information. Become as familiar as possible with the companies, jargon, topics covered and the industry as it is evolving.

OTHER IMPORTANT SOURCES OF INFORMATION

Trade associations are (generally nonprofit) organizations set up to advance the fortunes and concerns of a particular industry or profession. The membership of the American Association of Advertising Agencies (4A's), for example, is comprised of some 700-odd advertising agencies (including virtually all of the major ones) and dedicated to furthering the image of the advertising profession. Many trade associations publish newsletters and maintain research staffs. They are therefore an excellent source for industry data and statistics and may often have current information on employment trends and opportunities.

U.S. associations may be researched in the <u>Encyclopedia of Associations</u> (Gale Research Co.) or <u>National Trade and Professional Associations of the United States</u> (Columbia Books, Inc., 777 14th St., NW, Suite 236, Washington, DC 20005).

If you want to work for an association that serves a particular industry or profession, these same references will give you the information you need.

Job Fairs are informal get-togethers at which company recruiters and prospective employees can interact in a trade show-style atmosphere. The business section of your local paper will generally include announcements of those being held in your area.

ASK THE MAN WHO OWNS ONE

Some years ago, this advice was used as the theme for a highly successful automobile advertising campaign. The prospective car buyer was encouraged to find out about the product by asking the (supposedly) most trustworthy judge of all—someone who was already an owner.

You can use the same approach in your job search. You all have relatives or friends already out in the workplace—these are your best sources of information about those industries. Cast your net in as wide a circle as possible. Contact these valuable resources. You'll be amazed at how readily they will answer your questions. I suggest you check the criteria list at the beginning of this chapter to formulate your own list of pertinent questions. Ideally and minimally you will want to learn: how the industry is doing, what its long-term prospects are, the kinds of personalities they favor (aggressive, low key), rate of employee turnover and the availability of training.

THE UNDERSIDE OF THE ICEBERG

You are now better prepared to choose those industry groups that meet your own list of criteria. But a word of caution about these now-"obvious" requirements—they are not the only ones you need to take into consideration. And you probably won't be able to find all or many of the answers to this second set of questions in any reference book—they are known, however, by those persons already at work in the industry. Here is the list you will want to follow:

Promotion—If you are aggressive about your career plans, you'll want to know if you have a shot at the top job. Look for industries (and/or companies) that traditionally promote from within.

Training—Look for industries and companies in which your early tenure will actually be a period of on-the-job training, hopefully ones in which training remains part of the long-term process. As new techniques and technologies enter the workplace, you must make sure you are updated on these skills. Most importantly, look for training that is craft or function-oriented—these are the so-called **transferrable skills**, ones you can easily bring along with you from job-to-job, company-to-company, sometimes industry-to-industry.

Salary—Some industries are generally high-paying, some not. Though even an industry with a tradition of paying abnormally low salaries may have particular companies or job functions (like sales) within companies that command high remuneration. But it's important you know what the industry standard is.

Benefits—Look for industries in which health insurance, vacation pay, retirement plans, stock purchase opportunities and other important employee benefits are extensive…and company-paid. If you have to pay for basic benefits like medical coverage yourself, you'll be surprised at how expensive they are. An exceptional benefit package may even lead you to accept a lower-than-usual salary.

Unions—Make sure you know about the union situation in each industry you research. Periodic, union-mandated salary increases are one benefit non-union workers may find hard to match.

KEEP ON DIGGING

Research. It may be a new skill for you, but it's one you have to keep working on.

Now that you have a better idea of the industry in which you're interested, it's time to concentrate on particular companies and specific job/career areas (job functions). Chapter 3 will give you a well-designed blueprint on how to proceed.

CHAPTER THREE ✏

Corporate Culture And That "Just-Right" Company

This chapter shifts the focus of the job search process. Much of our previous discussion has concentrated on what *you* will bring to that process. Now we'll look at the other side of the coin—the company itself—and examine three important factors that may narrow your choices: the job description, the company profile and the corporate personality or culture. How these three factors are connected and how fundamentally they affect one another will soon become apparent. You will also see how they will affect the content and tone of your resume, as well as your approach to the interviewing process.

WHAT YOU ALREADY KNOW

As your research emphasis moves from the general (industry) to the more specific (company/job function), it's more important than ever to get into the habit of keeping detailed notes and records of what you discover along the way.

Based on what you've learned about yourself—your skills and capabilities and how they "match up" with those required by specific industries—and your detailed research into specific industries, you should already have a reasonably concrete idea of what you require in a company. While the discussion later in this chapter will further focus your preferences, let's start by recording what you already know.

Take another sheet of blank paper (yes, it's time for another list) and divide it into three vertical columns. Title it "My Ideal Company Profile." Call the left-hand column "Musts," the middle column "Preferences," and the right-hand column "Nevers."

We've listed a series of questions below. After considering each question, decide whether a particular criteria *must* be met, whether you would simply *prefer* it or *never* would consider it at all. If there are other criteria you consider important, feel free to add them to the list below and mark them accordingly on your Profile.

1. What are your geographical preferences? (Possible answers: U.S., Canada, International, Anywhere). If you only want to work in the U.S., then "Work in United States" would be the entry in the "Must" column. "Work in Canada or Foreign Country" might be the first entry in your "Never" column. There would be no applicable entry for this question in the "Preference" column. If, however, you will consider working in two of the three, then your "Must" column entry might read "Work in U.S. or Canada," your "Preference" entry—if you preferred one over the other—could read "Work in U.S.," and the "Never" column, "Work Overseas."

2. If you prefer to work in the U.S. or Canada, what area, state(s) or province(s)? If Overseas, what area or countries?

3. Do you prefer a large city, small city, town or somewhere as far away from civilization as possible?

4. In regard to question 3, any specific preferences?

5. Do you prefer a warm or cold climate?

6. Do you prefer a large or small company? Define your terms (by sales, income, employees, etc.).

7. Do you mind relocating right now? Do you want to work for a firm with a reputation for frequently relocating top people?

8. Do you mind travelling frequently? What percent do you consider reasonable?

9. What salary would you *like* to receive (put in the "Preference" column)? What's the *lowest* salary you'll accept (in the "Must" column)?

10. Are there any benefits (such as an expense account, medical and/or dental insurance, company car, etc.) you must or would like to have?

11. Are you planning to attend graduate school at some point in the future and, if so, is it important to you that a tuition reimbursement plan exist?

12. Do you feel a formal training program necessary?

13. What kinds of products or accounts would you prefer to work with?

It's important to keep revising this new form; after all, it contains the criteria by which you will judge every potential employer. It may even lead you to avoid interviewing at a specific company (if, for example, they're located in a state on your "never" list!). So be sure your "nevers" aren't frivolous. Likewise, make your "musts" and "preferences" at least semi-realistic. If your "must" salary for a position as an assistant researcher is $50,000, you may wind up eliminating every company out there!

CREATING YOUR COMMAND CHART

Here comes another chart, one we'll call your "Command Chart" or "Company Evaluation Chart." When completed, it will be the summary of all your research and contain all the information on the firms you've initially targeted. As you start networking, sending out resumes and cover letters, and preparing for interviews, you will find yourself constantly updating and referring to this Chart.

Create one vertical column down the left side—this is where you'll begin listing the companies you're considering. Then make as many columns across the top of the chart as you need to list all your "must" and "preference" criteria so you can "grade" them accordingly.

For example, using a list of possible entries on a hypothetical Company Profile, we would write in the following column headings and make an entry for each targeted firm in the appropriate space (from those possible, noted in parentheses):

1. STATE: List those you'll consider

2. CITY: Identify

3. COMPANY SIZE: By number of employees

4. FORMAL TRAINING PROGRAM: Check if "yes" and note important details—who's in charge, number of new trainees hired each year, etc.

5. BENEFITS: Leave enough room to list all company-wide benefits. Circle those especially important to you

6. TRAVEL: Enter percentage anticipated

7. SALARY: You'll probably want to leave this blank until able to enter a specific salary offer, but may want to include anything you discover about that company's general pay scales, etc.

Feel free to combine, add to, alter and use this new chart in any way that makes sense to you. While you should set up individual files for the companies high on your list (after "starring" the top ten or fifteen you like most), this Command Chart will remain an important form to refer back to. As we discuss new evaluation criteria later in this chapter, you may need to expand the Chart accordingly.

And remember that the many resources recommended in the previous chapter for industry research are the same references you will want to study to learn about specific companies.

40 WORDS OR LESS

Job descriptions are capsule summaries of a particular job function, its duties and responsibilities and the minimally-required education and skills to fill it. The Occupational Index, available in virtually every library, is a good basic reference for researching specific job titles and descriptions. Remember: Focus on the description; titles may vary wildly from company to company.

Job descriptions at each company are usually prepared by the Personnel department or by the specific person to whom you'll be reporting (in cooperation with the personnel staff).

The importance to *you* of such job descriptions should be obvious: They allow you to sort through and include or eliminate those career opportunities for which you are minimally qualified. And they can serve as a springboard for your preparation of the "Objective" section of your resume.

They will also help you differentiate between seemingly-similar job *titles* that, in reality, represent radically-different job *functions*...and discover seemingly-different job titles that actually require the same skills and represent the same duties and responsibilities.

To give you a better idea of what you're looking for, here are ten representative (and real) job titles and descriptions extracted from various company manuals:

Property Manager—Emphasis is on marketing, sales training and people skills. Should understand building maintenance procedures, rent collection, outside services coordination, elevator service and garbage collection. Tenant turnover requires selling skills for new rentals. Minimal hands-on skills for repair and service functions.

Employee Benefits Assistant—Assist in analyzing, designing and implementing employee benefits program under supervision of Director of Personnel Services. Adept at figures and cost analysis; must possess effective written and verbal communications skills. Some familiarity with liability, health and compensation insurance helpful. Computer familiarity desirable.

Sales Trainee—Excellent communications skills. Call on outside customers and set up appointments from furnished leads. Good administrative follow up, including correspondence and telemarketing activities. Responsive to structured sales approach.

Assistant Product Manager—Strong self-starter, well organized with economics/business degree. Assist in planning and implementing functions for major software product line sold to the automotive after-market field. Packaging, pricing, competitive analysis skills required.

Software Engineer—Degree in computer science and/or experience. Fluent in high-level computer languages. Knowledge of word processing, graphics, image processing, relational data bases. Ability to relate to non-technical personnel in a dynamic work environment.

Advertising Account Trainee—Degree in advertising, marketing or business administration. Knowledge of survey techniques, research, budget planning, long-range planning is desirable. Good people skills, high energy level. Flexible attitude and strong written communications skills mandatory.

Reporter—Strong grammarian and writer with excellent interviewing and analytical skills. Able to research and organize material and meet stringent deadlines. Ability to work on several different projects at one time is mandatory. Computer literate.

Inventory Control Clerk—Data entry skills for Kardex and computer system. Good numbers ability and systems understanding. Excellent administrative and clerical skills, typing and desk-top machine operations. Deadline oriented. Work with minimum supervision.

Paralegal—Excellent typing and dictation skills. Ability to research material through available library sources. Personable, articulate, presentable. Good people skills. Ability to work under pressure and relate to legal staff and client personnel.

Limousine Chauffeur—Perfect driving safety record—trucks, vans, public vehicles. Minimal English language, reading and writing skills. Presentable, courteous, able to work long hours with considerable overtime. Familiarity with major urban, suburban geography. State Motor Vehicle license #4.

It should be apparent that you can learn a lot from such job descriptions; they are usually very revealing of the attitudes of the corporation. And certain requirements tend to be included in each. We suggest you look for the following:

Practical skills—You can be certain you will not be considered unless you have them.

Hidden skills—For example, "people skills" where so noted. These are probably understated and may really be a very important part of the job function.

Educational credentials—When a certain degree or level of educational accomplishment is required, don't fabricate them. Rather, inquire whether work experience is an acceptable substitute.

Remember—job descriptions represent the *minimum* skills needed for consideration. Company personnel place a great deal of faith in them.

A LOOK TO THE FUTURE

Here's a peak at what lies ahead—those jobs that experts believe will be in greatest demand in the coming decades:

Hotel Management and Recreation: Check out what's happening in restaurants, resorts, travel and tourism and conference planning.

Food Service: From busboy to pastry chef, restaurants will need help. Food processing plants and food research laboratories are also good bets.

Basic Science: The U.S. must continue its drive to stay abreast of foreign competition. If your interest is in molecular biology, chemistry or optics, you're in good shape.

Computers: They will continue to exert an important force in all phases of daily life. Needs will be highest in design programming and maintenance.

Human Resources: As the work force continues to grow and employers seek greater efficiencies in their hiring practices, this area will grow, especially in the specialties of benefits planning, training, job evaluation and recruiting.

Teaching: Primary and secondary school teachers will be needed to serve on expanding population—the birthrate is trending upwards for the first time in many years. Math, science and foreign languages will be the important subject areas.

Maintenance Repair: Those of you good with your hands will have ample opportunity to demonstrate these skills.

GETTING TO KNOW THEM

As important as the objective resources outlined in the last chapter are, no book can tell you what it's really like to work at a specific company. So try to find out from the inside. Your best bet is to find and interview someone who works there. This will give you practical information—from someone already doing what you hope to be doing.

Barring that avenue, the company's annual report (or company brochure) usually contains detailed descriptive data. Don't take it as gospel—it is, after all, the way the company wants its publics to see it. But if you keep your grain of salt handy, the company profile included in its own promotional literature should give you two important pieces of information—what the company actually does and how it's doing.

I have reviewed many company profiles and distilled five representative ones below. All of the data was gleaned from public documents available to anyone (even you); company names have been omitted:

Stable, Steady, Private

Company A is a diversified corporation with operations in the Industrial Coated Fabrics, Polyurethane Foam, Apparel Textile and Consumer Product areas. It is a non-union operator with approximately 7,800 employees, doing business in four states and two foreign countries through 17 plants and sales offices.

Most products are resold to other manufacturers for their inclusion as components in end products. The Consumer Product Group markets, through retailers and chains, end products in the apparel area. Company has annual sales volume in excess of $300,000,000. Past three years profit performance has been satisfactory, with an annual pre-tax profit around 10%.

Until last year, Company's shares had been publicly traded, with annual shareholder dividends in the 8 - 9% range. A Management Group recently purchased the assets of the company in a bank/insurance company buy-back and has taken the company private. Considerable debt has been taken on to fund this move, and it is expected that costs will be trimmed to help finance this new debt and maintain earnings growth. Future growth for all divisions, with the exception of Apparel Textiles, is expected to be steady—textiles are beginning to feel the impact of low cost, low price competition from the Far East.

Management is stable, with major personnel averaging a ten-year tenure with the Company. Given the Company's family business origins, its record as an outstanding performer has been deliberately kept out of the spotlight. When questioned about the low profile, the Company's response was that it prefers to let its financial record speak for itself.

Aggressive New Management

Company B is an old-line, limited product company that has experienced tremendous growth because of the aggressive attitude of a new management team. Long active in the contract painting business, it developed a reputation for excellent performance, service and pricing, but profits were inordinately low.

Profits in the Paint Division have been improved by a new job bidding process, which has kept the Company away from low-bid work or work in which the profit potential was minimal.

The Company recently bought an office furniture company that it reorganized as a new Contract Furniture Division. Utilizing the considerable contacts in the real estate, building and construction industries developed by its Paint Division, it has rapidly expanded this new Division and, in the process, tripled the size of its business. It has also started an Electrostatic Refinishing and Design Division.

Employment has increased substantially, as has debt service on the new credit lines required to finance its expanded sales base. The Company has installed a centralized computer system.

Employee benefits—increased vacation time, profit sharing and promotion opportunities—have kept pace with growth. Some internal friction has been caused by the differences of style between the old company and its newly-acquired Division. Management is working this out through a program of inter-divisional transfer, with an incentive/bonus system that is perceived as fair to all employees.

Creating A Unique Niche

Company C has combined an aggressive, "finish the job ahead-of-schedule" attitude with a decentralized management style to fashion a distinctive niche in the construction sector of the environmental protection industry. As the low bidder on a major cleanup project at a hazardous waste site, its excellent performance quickly gained the attention of major state, federal and local authorities, whose impact in the construction business is considerable. Prison construction and bridge work soon followed.

The Company, as a pioneer in the waste material/hazardous waste sector, has been able to carve out a specialized niche which is mainly responsible for its current success.

The care and protection of workers on such jobs is an area in which the Company has developed significant expertise. Since few other firms have this experience, the Company has also been able to successfully market itself as a consultant on safety standards.

Current growth plans call for the establishment of a wholly-owned Canadian subsidiary, as well as the development of a real estate arm that will concentrate on motels and office buildings.

The Company is managed by a four-person Office of the President system, with each executive sharing power and responsibility. There is no Chief Executive Officer.

Organized For Growth

Company D is engaged in the franchising and building of low cost budget motels in 38 states. To date they have constructed in excess of 250 units and plan to add 100 units per year for the next three years. Its success is due to two primary factors: 1). its concentration in a growth industry sector—travel—and 2). an organizational structure that allows it to undercut the market.

Locating its units in small towns has protected it from major competition; its ability to offer a turnkey package (construction and motel-hotel supply) results in an unusually low cost per night rental. The Company's management believes that its subsidiary companies—which now include a property management unit and a telephone unit—make them particularly attractive to prospective franchisees, who often have little experience in these areas. The Company maintains that as long as it keeps its per-night price at the lowest end of the scale, it will continue to enjoy significant growth.

Company E manufactures high-quality, expensively-priced porcelain dolls. Started as a husband/wife weekend enterprise, the Company now sells its wares to major department stores and toy store retail outlets. It also does significant sales volume on a contract basis and enjoys licensing arrangements with major sports enterprise organizations. The production and design skills of the two principals allow the company to satisfy high-volume orders without sacrificing quality, the key to its ability to succeed in the fast-paced retail environment.

If information as detailed as this is available on such a variety of different companies, is there any reason to *not* know such data before *you* walk into an interview situation? Of course not! And remember: This is not information unearthed after weeks in the library; all of it was obtained just by reading a couple of pages of each company's own promotional literature.

TIME FOR A BREAK

Just a reminder of the importance of record-keeping, one of the fundamentals of the job search process. Once you have written your resume, your ability to follow up during the job search and interview process will be critical to success. So a word to the wise: Record keeping will be important. In the following two chapters, I'll demonstrate two simple systems you can use to stay on top of the search—the card file and spread sheet methods.

WHYS & WHEREFORES OF CORPORATE CULTURE

The Introduction presented the concept of **corporate culture**, an acknowledgement that different companies have different styles or "personalities." Though such inherent differences between companies have, of course, always existed, they were seen as one-sided influences—employees could either take them or leave them—so no one bothered to single them out for further inspection.

Today's work force is more independent, so further investigation into this phenomenon is appropriate. The company's physical environment, your co-workers and management's attitude and policies are all part and parcel of each company's culture. Remember: You're looking for a company environment in which you'll fit and feel comfortable, a place at which you'd enjoy working. The following key factors are good barometers of the kind of company you're about to get yourself into. Check your own preliminary list of companies and see where each fits.

One Man/Family Rule

Some companies are dominated by a single personality, either a still-active founder or an executive who has exerted an unusually strong or long-standing influence on the company's rise to prominence. While there are exceptions, such companies tend to be "closely-held" fiefdoms that feature an autocratic management style. (The exceptions feature benign despots who, despite their more charitable ways, still rule.) All decisions, even the smallest, filter down from the executive mountaintop. There is little room for individual initiative and a cult of personality usually prevails. This can be understandably disconcerting for talented individuals seeking responsibility and autonomy. (The opposite of such a company is a decentralized one, in which each department or division takes responsibility for its own bottom line and subordinates are regularly included in decision-making.)

A family-owned company may promise similar problems. Not only may your chance to make decisions and take responsibility be tied to your last name, so may any chance of making it to the top. Barely competent family members may wind up with cushy jobs and high pay, while you and other "outsiders" do all the work. While many such firms are privately-held, even publicly-traded companies in which family members hold the majority of stock only have to answer to the family. And what's good for the family might have little to do with what's good for you...or even for the company.

The Pseudo-Darwinian Cage

The efficiency of the Japanese, as manifested in the cult status of their "Theory Z" management style with its emphasis on consensus building, has certainly underscored the futility of an adversarial relationship in the workplace. Competition should be focused on the task to be achieved and against other rivals in the marketplace, not other rivals within the company.

Unfortunately, such is not usually the case. If a "we vs. they" mentality exists between workers and management or if managers regularly spend half their time politicking or writing self-serving memos to the boss, it's a survival-of-the-fittest (or survival-of-the-best-memo-writer) atmosphere. People attuned to corporate infighting might relish such a company; those who just want to do their jobs and be rewarded for the work they do tend to find it an unfriendly place to work.

High Key, Low Key, No Key

Some companies are fairly bursting with energy; their offices seem to reverberate with a steady hum of activity. Such a **high-key** environment. is right for aggressive go-getters ready to jump into the fray, unafraid of such a fast pace.

Other work places are calm, quiet, almost studious in nature. Such **low-key** firms are probably better choices for less-hectic personalities.

While a high- or low-key atmosphere says little about a particular company's chance for success, it may have a lot to do with your own on-the-job performance, success and happiness. Matching dissimilar corporate and individual personalities usually results in a new job search.

If you run across a company that seems to give off no signals at all, then danger lurks. This is usually the directionless organization that just seems to be floating along in the corporate seas. More often than not, no one is in charge, no one is setting the pace or agenda for the organization. Without such leadership, you can be certain that sooner or later this organization will founder, usually when things start going wrong and the timely implementation of company-wide decisions is required.

Feeling Lucky?

Let's pretend for a moment: You have been hired as a computer programmer for a prestigious engineering firm. Your first day on the job, several things happen almost at once: 1). You are told that for your first week you will be assigned to the new employee training sessions sponsored by the Personnel department; 2). a multi-page folder titled "Employee Benefits And Work Policies " is dropped on your desk; and 3). you are invited to a Friday after-work cocktail party in the company cafeteria.

We suggest you thank your lucky stars—or perhaps the research hours spent in investigation of just such things. This is a company that obviously cares about its employees and has made a commitment to train them, care for their needs and make them feel at home. It's the kind of corporate culture you should be looking for.

CHAPTER FOUR ✏

That's What Friends Are For

Networking is a term you have probably heard; it is definitely a key aspect of any successful job search and a process you must master. **Informational interviews** and **job interviews** are the two primary outgrowths of successful networking. **Referrals,** an aspect of the networking process, entail using someone else's name, credentials and recommendation to set up a receptive environment when seeking a job interview. All of these terms have one thing in common: Each depends on the actions of other people to put them in motion.

So what *is* networking? *How* do you build your own network? And *why* do you need one in the first place? This chapter answers all of those questions and more.

AN AGE-OLD SYSTEM

As Gekko, the high-rolling corporate raider, sneers in the movie <u>Wall Street,</u> "Any schmuck can analyze stock charts. What separates the players from the sheep is **information**." Networking is the process of creating your own group of relatives, friends and acquaintances who can feed you the information *you* need to find a job—identifying where the jobs are and giving you the personal introductions and background data necessary to pursue them. If the job market were so well-organized that details on all employment opportunities were immediately available to all applicants, there would be no need for such a process. Rest assured the job market is *not* such a smooth-running machine —most applicants are left very much to their own devices. Build and use your own network wisely and you'll be amazed at the amount of useful job intelligence it will turn up for you.

While the term networking didn't gain prominence until the 1970s, it is by no means a new phenomenon. A selection process that connects people of similar skills, backgrounds and/or attitudes—in other words, networking—has been in existence in a variety of forms for centuries. Attend any Ivy League school and you're automatically part of its centuries-old network. A so-called Old Boys Network has been at work in this country for years, especially in the selection of presidential candidates. (As a result, a single New England prep school has numbered among its graduates a disproportionate number of inhabitants of the Oval Office.)

Major law firms are known to favor candidates from a preferred list of law schools—the same ones the senior partners attended. Washington, D.C. and Corporate America have their own network—the same corporate bigwigs move back and forth from boardroom to Cabinet Room. The Academia-Washington connection is just as strong—notice the number of Harvard professors (e.g., Henry Kissinger, John Kenneth Galbraith) who call Washington their second home? No matter which party is in power, certain names just keep surfacing as Secretary of This or Undersecretary of That.

No, networking is not new. It's just left its ivory tower and become a well-publicized process *anyone* can and should utilize in their lifelong career development.

And it works. Remember your own reaction when you were asked to recommend someone for a job, club or school office? You certainly didn't want to look foolish, so you gave it some thought and tried to recommend the best-qualified person that would "fit in" with the rest of the group. It's a built-in screening process—what's more natural than recommending someone who's "our kind of _____?"

CREATING THE IDEAL NETWORK

As in most endeavors, there's a wrong way and a right way to network. The following tips will help you construct a wide-ranging, information-gathering, interview-generating group—your very own network.

Diversify

Unlike the Harvard or Princeton network—confined to former graduates of each school—*your* network should be as diversified and wide-ranging as possible. You never know who might be in a position to help, so don't limit your group of friends. The more diverse they are, the greater the variety of information they may supply you with.

Don't Forget...

...to include everyone you know in your initial networking list: friends, relatives, social acquaintances, classmates, college alumni, professors, teachers; your dentist, doctor, family lawyer, insurance agent, banker, travel agent; elected officials in your community; ministers; fellow church members; local tradesmen; local business or social club officers. And everybody *they* know!

Be Specific

Make a list of the kinds of assistance you will require from those in your network, then make specific requests of each. Do they know of jobs at their company? Can they introduce you to the proper executives? Have they heard something about or know someone at the company you're planning to interview with next week?

The more organized you are, the easier it will be to target the information you need and figure out who might have it. Calling everyone and simply asking for "whatever help you can give me" is unfair to the people you're calling and a less-effective way to garner the information you need.

Know The Difference...

...between an **informational** interview and a **job** interview. The former requires you to cast yourself in the role of information-gatherer; *you* are the interviewer and knowledge is your goal—about an industry, company, job function, key executive, etc. Such a meeting with someone already doing what you soon *hope* to be doing is by far the best way to find out everything you need to know...before you walk through the door and sit down for a formal job interview, at which time your purpose is more sharply-defined: to get the job you're interviewing for.

If you learn of a specific job opening during an informational interview, you are in a position to find out details about the job, identify the interviewer and, possibly, even learn some things about him or her. In addition, presuming you get your contact's permission, you may be able to use his or her name as a referral. Calling up the interviewer and saying, "Joan Smith in your New Accounts department suggested I contact you regarding openings for assistant bank tellers," is far superior to "Hello. Do you have any job openings in your bank?"

(In such a case, be careful about referring to a specific job opening, even if your contact told you about it. It may not be something you're supposed to know about. By presenting your query as an open-ended question, you give your prospective employer the option of exploring your background without further commitment. If there is a job there and you're qualified for it, you'll find out soon enough.)

Don't Waste A Contact

Not everyone you call on your highly-diversified networking list will know about a job opening. It would be surprising if each one did. But what about *their* friends and colleagues? It's amazing how everyone knows someone who knows someone. Ask—you'll find that someone.

Value Your Contacts

If you've taken our admonitions about record keeping to heart, this is where you'll begin to appreciate the dividends. If someone has provided you with helpful information or an introduction to a friend or colleague, keep him or her informed about how it all turns out. A referral that's panned out should be reported to the person who opened the door for you in the first place. Such courtesy will be appreciated...and may lead to more contacts. If someone has nothing to offer today, a call back in the future is still appropriate and may yet pay off.

The lesson is clear: Keep your options open and your contact list alive. Keeping detailed records of your network—who you spoke with, when, what transpired, etc.—will certainly help you keep track of your overall progress and organize what can be a complicated and involved process.

CONDUCTING AN INFORMATIONAL INTERVIEW

You were, of course, smart enough to include John Fredericks, the bank officer who handled your dad's mortgage, on your original contact list. He knew you as a bright and concientious college senior; in fact, your perfect three-year repayment record on the loan you took out to buy that '67 Plymouth impressed him. When you called him, he was happy to refer you to his friend, Bob Jones, Director of MIS (Management Information Systems) at XYZ Corp. Armed with permission to use Fredericks' name and recommendation, you wrote a letter to Bob Jones, the gist of which went something like this:

"I am writing at the suggestion of Mr. Fredericks at Fidelity National Bank. He knows of my interest in the computer programming field and, given your position at XYZ, thought you may be able to help me get a clearer understanding of it and how I might eventually be able to fit in.

While I am taking advanced courses in computer sciences, I know I need to speak with professionals such as yourself to get a better understanding of the "big picture."If you could spare a half hour to meet with me, I'm certain I would be able to get enough information about this specialty to give me the direction I need.

I'll call your office next week in the hope that we can schedule a meeting."

Send a copy of this letter to Mr. Fredericks at the bank—it will refresh his memory should Mr. Jones call to inqure about you. Next step: the follow-up phone call. After you get Mr. Jones' secretary on the line, it will, with luck, go something like this:

"Hello, I'm Mr. Paul Smith. I'm calling in reference to a letter I wrote to Mr. Jones requesting an appointment."

"Oh, yes. You're the young man interested in computer programming. Mr. Jones can see you on June 23rd. Will 10 A.M. be satisfactory?"

"That's fine. I'll be there."

Well the appointed day arrives. Well-scrubbed and dressed in your best (and most conservative) suit, you are ushered into Mr. Jones' office. He offers you coffee (you decline) and says that it is okay to light up if you wish to smoke (you decline). The conversation might go something like this:

You: "Thank you for seeing me, Mr. Jones. I know you are busy and appreciate your taking the time to talk with me."

Jones: "Well it's my pleasure since you come so highly recommended. I'm always pleased to meet someone interested in my field. You college-trained computer people are our resevoir of future programmers."

You: "As I stated in my letter, my interest in computers is very real, but I'm having trouble seeing how all of my studies fit into the big picture. I think I'll be much better prepared to evaluate future job offers if I can learn how everything fits. May I ask you a few questions about the computer function at XYZ company?"

Mr. Jones relaxes. He realizes this is a knowledge hunt you are on, not a thinly-veiled job interview. Your approach has kept him off the spot—he doesn't have to be concerned with making a hiring decision. You've already gotten high marks for not putting him on the defensive.

Jones: "Fire away, Paul".

You: "I have a few specific questions I'd like to ask. First, how is the computer function organized?"

Jones: "In this company we work on a centralized basis. All operating departments funnel their requests for computer work through the Information Systems Department."

You: "Do you feel this limits the opportunities for career advancement into other areas of the company?"

Jones: "No, we make a special effort to see that all personnel understand the functions of each of our departments. Many programmers have ended up in Engineering, others in Administration."

You: "What is the work environment like—is it pretty hectic?"

Jones: "We try to keep the work load at an even keel. The comfort of our workers is of prime importance to us. Excessive turnover is costly, you know."

You: "If I may shift to another area, I'd be interested in your opinion about the computer field in general and what you see as the most likely areas of opportunity in the forseeable future. Do you think this is a growth career area?"

Jones: "Well, judging by the hiring record of our company, I think you'll find it's an area worth making a committment to. At the entry level, we've hired fourteen new programmers in each of the past three years. There always seems to be data to collect and analyze."

You: "How would someone with my qualifications and background get started in the computer area? Perhaps a look at my resume. would be helpful to you." (Give Mr. Jones your resume.)

Jones: "We start our entry-level employees in data entry, then move them on to analysis and program development, a progression I think you'll find is relatively common among companies our size. I think these courses you've taken would more than qualify you for such a position."

You: "You have been very generous with your time, but I can see from those flashing buttons on your phone that you have have other things to do. Are there other individuals at XYZ or in the industry you think I should talk with?" (Write down names and phone numbers.) "Thank you again."

AFTER THE INTERVIEW

The next step should be obvious: <u>Two</u> thank-you letters are required, one to Mr. Jones, the second to Mr. Fredericks. Get them both out immediately. (And see chapter 8 if you need help writing them.)

Keeping Track of The Interview Trail

Let's talk about record keeping again. If your networking works the way it's supposed to, this was only the first of many such interviews. Experts have estimated that the average person could develop a contact list of 250 people. Even if we limit your initial list to only 100, if each of them gave you one referral, your list would suddenly have 200 names. Presuming that it will not be necessary or helpful to see all of them, it's certainly possible that such a list could lead to 100 informational and/or job interviews! Unless you keep accurate records, by the time you're on No. 50, you won't even remember the first dozen!

So get the results of each interview down on paper. Use whatever format you're comfortable with. You should create some kind of file, folder or note card that is an "Interview Recap Record." It should be set up and contain something like the following:

Name: XYZ Company
Address: 22 Sheridan Place, Elmira, N.Y. 10029
Phone: (607) 516-82#5
Contact: Robert L. Jones
Type of Business: Aircraft Engine Manufacturer
Referral Contact: Mr. Fredericks, Fidelity National Bank
Date: June 23, 1987

At this point, you should add a one- or two-paragraph summary of what you found out at the meeting. Since these comments are for your eyes only, you should be both objective and subjective. State the facts—what you found out in response to your specific questions—but include your impressions—your estimate of the opportunities for further discussions, your chances for future consideration for employment. The following is what we'd include about XYZ Corp:

"XYZ looks to college-trained personnel to fill their entry-level computer slots. Operations are centralized—all computer work goes through the Information Systems Department. Company emphasizes full employee understanding of all facets of the company's operations and encourages lateral, interdepartment transfers. Work environment is low key. High turnover is seen as being undesireable because it is so costly to train and indoctrinate new people. Computers are seen as a growth area based on the company's prior hiring record and the continuing flow of new information and data. Mr. Jones seemed impressed with my resume and general presentation. I could tell from the pictures on his office wall that he is an outdoors type (so am I). XYZ's offices seemed neat, well lit and quiet. I think a person could get a lot of work done there. Their computer equipment is state of the art. "

"I Was Just Calling To..."

Find any logical opportunity to stay in touch with Mr. Jones. You may, for example, let him know when you graduate and tell him your Grade Point Average, carbon him on any letters you write to Mr. Fredericks, even send a congratulatory note if his company's year-end financial results are positive or if you read something in the local paper about his department. This type of follow up has the all-important effect of keeping you and your name in the forefront of others' minds. Out of sight *is* out of mind. No matter how talented you may be or how good an impression you made, you'll have to work hard to "stay visible."

THE RULES OF THE GAME

It should already be obvious that the networking process is not only effective, but also quite deliberate in its objectives. There are two specific groups of people you must attempt to target: those who can give you information about an industry or career area and those who are potential employers. The line between these groups may often blur. Don't be concerned—you'll soon learn when (and how) to shift the focus from interviewer to interviewee.

To simplify this process, follow a single rule: Show interest in the industry or job area under discussion, but wait to be asked about actually working for that company. During your informational interviews, you will be surprised at the number of times the person you're interviewing turns to you and asks, "Would you be interested in...?" Consider carefully what's being asked and, if you *would* be interested in the position under discussion, make your feelings known.

A SUMMARY OF YOUR OBJECTIVES

- To unearth current information about the industry, company and pertinent job functions. Remember: Your knowledge and understanding of broad industry trends, financial health, hiring opportunities and the competitive picture are key.

- To investigate each company's hiring policies—who makes the decisions, who the key players are (personnel, staff managers), whether there's a hiring season, whether they prefer applicants going direct or through recruiters, etc.

- To sell yourself—discuss your interests and research activities —and leave yur calling card, your resume.

- To seek out advice on refining your job search process.

- To obtain the names of other persons (referrals) who can give you additional information on where the jobs are and what the market conditions are like.

- To develop a list of follow-up activities that will keep you visible to key contacts.

IF THE PROCESS SCARES YOU

Some of you will undoutedly be hesitant about, even fear, the networking process. It is not an unusual response—it is very human to want to accomplish things "on your own," without anyone's help. Understandable and commendable as such independence might seem, it is, in reality, an impediment if it limits your involvement in this important process. Networking has such universal application because *there is no other effective way to*

bridge the gap between job applicant and job. Employers are grateful for its existence. You should be, too.

Whether you are a first-time applicant or reentering the work force now that the children are grown, the networking process will more than likely be your point of entry. Sending out mass mailings of your resume and answering the help-wanted ads may well be less personal (and, therefore, "easier") approaches, but they will also be far less effective. The natural selection process of the networking phenomenon is your assurance that water does indeed seek its own level—you will be matched up with companies and job opportunities in which there is a mutual fit.

SIX GOOD REASONS TO NETWORK

Many people fear the networking process because they think they are "bothering" others with their own selfish demands. Humbug! There are good reasons—six of them, at least—why the people on your networking list will be *happy* to help you:

1). ***Some day you will get to return the favor.*** An ace insurance salesman built a successful business by offering low-cost coverage to first-year medical students. Ten years later, these now-successful practitioners remembered the company (and person) that helped them when they were just getting started. He gets new referrals every day.

2). ***They, too, are seeking information.*** If you sense that your "brain is being picked" about the latest techniques of computer graphics, be forthcoming with your information. Schools and universities are often at the forefront of technology, so why not let the interviewer "audit" your course? It may be the reason he or she agreed to see you in the first place.

3). ***Internal politics***—Some people will see you simply to make themselves appear powerful, implying to others in their organization that they have the authority to hire (they may or may not), an envied prerogative.

4). ***They're "saving for a rainy day"***—Executives know that it never hurts to look and that maintaining a backlog of qualified candidates is a big asset when the floodgates open and supervisors are forced to hire quickly.

5). ***They're just plain nice***—Some people will see you simply because they feel it's the decent thing to do or because they just can't say "no."

6) ***They are looking themselves***—Some people will see you because they are anxious to do a friend (whoever referred you) a favor. Or because they have another friend seeking new talent, in which case you represent a referral *they* can make (part of their own continuing network process). You see, networking never *does* stop—it helps them and it helps you.

Before you proceed to Chapter 5, begin making your contact list. You may wish to keep a separate sheet of paper or note card on each person (especially the dozen or so you think are most important), even a separate telephone list to make your communications easier and more efficient. However you set up your list, be sure to keep it up to date—it won't be long before you'll be calling each and every name on the list.

CHAPTER FIVE ✐

A Place For Everything

One surefire way of expanding your network of contacts is to take advantage of the public and private employment services already in place in your community: the employment and counseling services that are part of the Federal government (and most state and local governments) and the array of recruiters, counselors and employment agencies who specialize in job placement. However broad and varied your own network, there is certainly no reason not to add such companies and agencies to your list—it is estimated that between 7% and 10% of all successful job searches go through these channels.Many firms use these agencies as screening devices because there is no fee to the employer. It will require a good deal of running around on your part, but the energy you'll expend will be worth it. The key point to remember is that these organizations *do* have jobs they are seeking to fill.

THE STATE WANTS YOU

From a recent <u>State Announcement Of Opportunities In Government</u>:

<u>Position</u>: Public Information Specialist.
<u>Starting Salary</u>: $21,000.
Written test required.
<u>Job Description and Minimum Qualifications</u>: Engage in the preparation of written material, editing and dissem-

ination of informational materials concerning the programs and activities of a State agency through various media including: newspapers, radio, tv, motion pictures, periodicals and state publications. Proof of work experience and work samples will be required prior to test admission. Education may be substituted for experience as follows: a bachelors degree in a relevant field (this includes courses and major emphasis in journalism, advertising, communications, radio and tv).

Test Details: a multiple choice and essay section are included in the test for this position. Successful scores may qualify the applicant for an oral test section.

Fees: There is a $5 filing fee to take this examination which must be included with the application."

Though a friend had to wait approximately six months for a chance at this job (and the job *did* come through), it was a well-invested five dollars. Competitive examinations give you the advantage of going after positions in which your experience and education can pay off. There is far less focus on your personality—and more on specific qualifications—than in the private sector. If you are well trained, possess the requisite skills and/or education and are comfortable with and tend to do well on tests, I would suggest you locate and enter as many of these competitions as possible.

OPEN SEASON ON YOU

Two other potential resources for job leads are the **employment agency**, to which you may have to pay a fee, and **recruiters**. Either or both may be retained by companies to screen candidates for particular job openings. Both types of firms can be found in your local Yellow Pages under the headings "Employment Agencies," "Vocational Guidance" and/or "Executive Recruiting Firms."

How do these two types of "screening" firms differ? Employment agencies typically survive on high volume—lots of job openings in lots of industries. While many of these *are* entry-level opportunities, they are invariably clerical or secretarial. If that's the kind of position you are seeking, your local employment agency should be a first stop.

If you are hoping for a position that has more potential to lead you up the career ladder, the executive recruiter, who plays a more discriminating role for his or her client companies, is your best bet. Recruiting firms often specialize in a single industry—the principals have probably parlayed their own work experience in a given industry into extensive knowledge of the job requirements in that field. Many have worked in the Human Resources or Personnel departments of major corporations; it's a short leap from recruiting for a single company to recruiting the same types of people for the same types of jobs in a single industry.

Since recruiters generally charge their clients a higher fee than general employment agencies, companies tend to use them for harder-to-fill executive slots, not entry-level positions. Of course, there are always exceptions and you would be advised to at least inquire at any local recruiting firms for potential openings that require little or no experience. You can secure a list of recruiting firms by writing for a copy of the <u>Executive Employment Guide</u>, available from the American Management Association (135 West 50th St., New York, N.Y. 10020).

If you plan to work with either type firm, make sure you:

• **Don't just saunter into the local employment agency or recruiter**—make every effort to be referred by a friend or acquaintance who found employment through that organization. The networking skills you've developed will surely help you here.

• **Work with only one organization in each industry or specialization.** If a company receives your resume from three different agencies, it is already apparent to them that you are "shotgunning" the field, hoping to hit a target, *any* target. You don't want to leave such an impression; rather, you hope the discrimination you show in your own job search will identify you as a selective, targeted job hunter who knows what he or she wants.

• **Try to establish a close relationship with the organization and individual with whom you work.** If he or she gets you a job, and you are successful at it, you can be certain you'll be on his or her list when future opportunities arise. But if you refer friends and colleagues to that firm, you will have established an important debt—they'll owe *you!*—that will ensure the pick of those opportunities.

LET YOUR FINGERS DO THE WALKING

The remainder of this chapter will review a host of sources you can access to get the job lead information you need. But don't overlook the most obvious source of all—your local telephone directory. To demonstrate how helpful it can be, here are just some of the pertinent listings I found in the New York City Yellow Pages:

State, Federal, Municipal Civil Service
State Labor Department Employment Services
Federal Job Information Center
State Jobs:
      Household
      Industrial Construction and Transportation
      Office Personnel
      Professional Placement
U.S. Office Of Personnel Management

City Summer Youth Employment Program
Veterans Administration
Community Development Agency
The Mayor's Office Of the Handicapped
Neighborhood Manpower Service Center
Employment Agencies/Recruiters (19 pages of listings)

Take a moment to review your own local telephone directories. Make another list and place it in your Resources file for future reference. Adept researcher that you are, you'll know when and how to use it.

ON WITH THE SEARCH

Down to the nitty-gritty—a listing and assessment of the most valuable resources that can be found in most cities. If you live in a major city—New York, Los Angeles, Dallas, etc.—the facilities available to you will be greater in number and scope. So if you are a small-town resident, it'd be worth a few calls, even a trip or two, to the largest metropolitan center in your area.

State Employment Agencies

As indicated earlier in this chapter, state laws mandate that these offices make all job openings known to everyone. You'll find them displayed on their office bulletin boards.

Civil service jobs offered by your state may well be advertised in specialty publications available at local newsstands. Most competitive examination job openings are also listed in such periodicals. (My friend who landed the Public Information Officer position learned of it through just such a listing.)

State Labor Department Unemployment/Outplacement Centers are also sources of job leads—many good job openings are in their computer files. Savvy employers know that many unemployed persons are in that condition through no fault of their own and are anxiously seeking work—they place a high value on this pool of talent (especially since they don't have to pay private agency fees!).

You usually do *not* have to be receiving unemployment benefits to qualify or apply for such jobs. Inquire at the Unemployment Office in your area.

Job Information Centers

Since you should be spending a lot of time in your local library anyway, researching industries, companies and job functions, the next time you're there see if they have a section that acts as a job clearing center. Many employers list jobs with these centers—the bulletin board is the primary "ad"—and many libraries have knowledgeable counselors on staff who are invaluable sources of information and assistance.

Human Services Agencies

As the Federal government continues to de-emphasize its role in the delivery of social services, many states, counties and cities have taken over such efforts. And many private groups have stepped up their work in these areas. Send inquiries to the headquarters of the Human or Social Services organizations in each city for the various women's groups, social service organizations, rehabilitation centers, etc. set up in your area.

Veteran's Organizations

If you qualify, you can get a good deal of job information (and preferential treatment because of your status) through such centers. The Veteran's Administration (based in Washington, D.C.) can give you a list of federally-funded branches and information on privately-funded veteran's groups in your city or area. And don't forget your local chapters of the American Legion or Veterans of Foreign Wars (VFW).

College Placement And High School Guidance Offices

If you are a college graduate—or plan to be one soon—by all means take advantage of the Career Counseling, Job Placement or Career Resource Center at your school. Employers are always in touch with them; many actively recruit on campus. If you are interested in a particular company that is scheduling an on-campus visit, get in touch with the advisor at your college and make sure you get on his or her interview list.

The help available through high school guidance offices is often more limited, as a good part of their effort is directed to students going on to college. Since opportunities for high school graduates are more limited, they tend to concentrate their employment efforts in the vocational, clerical and so-called trade areas open to those students not planning to attend a four-year college.

Community And Junior Colleges

These schools have become particularly valuable to certain employers because they produce candidates whose skills and interests are highly-targeted. Companies in technical fields such as computers or electronics—where mastery of English literature and Medieval history is not a prime prerequisite—are especially aware of the competent graduates such two-year colleges turn out and usually stay in close contact with those in their local area.

Trade, Technical And Business Schools

Secretarial, bartending, barber, beauty, tv repair, computer programming schools and the like: If you have decided on such a trade, the training and job placement most good schools in these specialties offer are probably worth the tuition. Before you pay your money, though, make sure you check out such trade schools with the local Better Business Bureau—while virtually all four- and two-year colleges can be trusted to deliver what they promise, there have been enough instances of "fly-by-night" trade institutes to make a smart consumer take pause before he or she pays the sometimes-hefty tuition.

GETTING THE MOST OUT OF YOUR RESOURCES

How to deal with the various people you'll meet as you tap these public and private resources is a skill well worth learning. Here are some time-tested tips to keep in mind as you prepare to deal with the employment bureaucracy:

• Make sure you know the difference between a **custodian of information** and a **counselor**—you will, hopefully, be seeking more of the former than the latter. Government personnel all too often work by the book. Limited incentive and restrictive disciplinary practices can be corrosive to performance. So if you think the person you are dealing with is doing the absolute minimum and offering nothing if not asked...repeatedly...he or she probably is. The trick is to know what each organization has to offer and how to work with each personality-type you encounter to successful dig it out.

• *Be courteous.* There may well be a good deal of tedium and routine in the jobs that these personnel are asked to do. A smile and a good word may make their day...and be their incentive to make *yours*, by promptly giving you the information you require.

• *Be persistent:* If you don't get the information you need the first time around, don't be afraid to go back or to try another person in the same office. There is a considerable amount of shifting of such personnel and an abundance of part-time help (who *may* know the location of the rest rooms, but little else!) If you are sure the answer you require lurks somewhere in that office, keep searching for the person who knows it...and keep asking him or her until you get it.

• When seeking advice from counselors at employment agencies and recruiting organizations, avoid the fast-acting, fill-the-job personality-types. They are rarely concerned about *your* objectives, only about what (or who) they can sell to a prospective employer. These are the "body snatcher, head hunter" types you may already have heard about. Look for the recruiter or agent who displays a genuine interest in you. The more questions he or she asks of you—the deeper into your educational and work background the probe goes—the better off you will be.

WHAT DO YOU KNOW? AND WHEN DID YOU KNOW IT?

It's been nearly 70 pages, and we've barely mentioned the word "resume." But, at last, it's time to go on to the active steps these 70 pages have been leading up to: preparing your resume, drafting cover and thank-you letters, interviewing and testing.

Your friends who weren't as smart as you were—they failed to buy this book!—are perhaps well into this process already. Have you fallen behind?

Not at all! The detailed research you have accomplished, the skills you have begun to develop and the exhausting preparatory work you have undertaken are the basis of the job-search process. They are the brick and mortar—the solid foundation—that will make these latter steps seem almost easy by comparison.

And they should be—you've already *done* the hard work.

So sharpen your pencil, and let's finally start using all that research you've done to make a resume.

CHAPTER SIX ✎

You're Ready To Write Your Resume

By this stage in your job search, certain things about your capabilities should be obvious: You possess particular skills, may well have some work experience, and are educated, intelligent, diligent and a reader (you've gotten this far in the book, haven't you?).

But you may not be a *writer,* and that's what's scaring you about your resume. Take heart—you don't *have* to be the incarnation of Hemingway to create an effective, selling resume. Only about 177 words (excluding headings) stand between you and the completion of your resume, not a lot of writing by anyone's standards (though it may seem like a lot!). By the time you are finished with this chapter, you'll have mastered everything you need to know to make it easy.

AN OVERVIEW OF RESUME PREPARATION

• **Know what you're doing**—your resume is a personal billboard of accomplishments. It must communicate your worth to a prospective employer in specific terms.

• **Your language should be action-oriented,** full of "doing"-type words. And less is better than more—be concise and direct. Don't worry about using complete sentences.

• **Be persuasive.** In those sections that allow you the freedom to do so, don't hesitate to communicate your worth in the strongest language. This does not mean a numbing list of self-congratulatory superlatives; it does mean truthful claims about your abilities and the evidence (educational, experiential) that supports them.

• **Don't be cheap or gaudy.** Don't hesitate to spend the few extra dollars necessary to present a professional-looking resume. Do avoid outlandish (and generally ineffective) gimmicks like over-sized or brightly-colored paper.

• **Find an editor.** Every good writer needs one, and you are writing your resume. At the very least, it will offer you a second set of eyes proofreading for embarassing typos. But if you are fortunate enough to have a professional in the field—a recruiter or personnel executive—critique a draft, grab the opportunty and be immensely grateful.

• **If you're the next Michaelangelo,** so multi-talented that you can easily qualify for jobs in different career areas, don't hesitate to prepare two or more completely different resumes. This will enable you to change the emphasis on your education and skills according to the specific career objective on each resume, a necessary alteration that will corectly target each one.

• **Choose the proper format.** There are only three we recommend—chronological, functional and combination—and it's important you use the one that's right for you.

THE RECORDS YOU NEED

Despite the chapter title, you're actually *almost* ready to write your resume. First, you have to make sure you have assembled and organized all the records you need.

The reason for organizing records is to be more efficient and accurate when you sit down to prepare the ingredients for your resume. Records do NOT belong scattered throughout the household or dumped into the family "record file" in a kitchen drawer. Organizing your records in a single location, filed by topic, will save you time, energy and stress.

So start by deciding upon a single location in which to store your personal records. Develop a good filing system and, if you don't own a file cabinet, consider buying one of two products available at most stationery or office supply stores: an expandable pocket portfolio or a solid plastic file box (sturdier, but less compact). In either container, designate a separate folder for each of the following categories of important documents:

• **REPORT CARDS**

Along with actual report cards, you might save samples of your work—especially in courses pertinent to your career objective. The actual work easily records interests, talents, difficulties and accomplishments. Work samples will also come in handy when you request letters of recommendation from past employers.

• TRANSCRIPTS/GPA/CLASS RANK

Transcripts are your school's official record of your academic history. They are generally kept in the guidance office (high school) or registrar's office (college). Make sure honors courses are noted in the transcript.

The GPA (Grade Point Average) is usually found on the transcript. Many schools generally calculate this by computing credits times a numerical grade equivalent (often "A" = 4.0, "B" = 3.0, etc.). Class rank is simply a listing of GPAs, from highest to lowest. Example: 75/306 (75th out of a class of 306 students).

• ACTIVITY RECORDS

This should be a comprehensive list of sports, music and other extra-curricular or special activities in which you've participated, either inside or outside school. (In the next section, we've included a Data Input Sheet that will allow you to organize all this information.)

• AWARDS/HONORS

List award name, date received and significance of the award. Example: Peabody Scholar, 1987, awarded to Jefferson High School senior who demonstrates musical prowess and an interest in pursuing a musical career.

• WORK/VOLUNTEER RECORDS

List each job title, dates of employment, business address, responsibilities. Any work experience, from babysitting to lawn mowing, should be listed. Also list any volunteer work, even if it was only for one day.

• MILITARY RECORDS

Include complete military history, if pertinent.

• TRAVEL RECORDS

Keep a list of your travel experiences and, perhaps, some personal reactions to each trip. Travel experience helps demonstrate that you are well-rounded, and the written reactions might prompt responses to interview questions.

THIS IS NOT THE TIME OR PLACE TO BE MODEST! Keep track of all your accomplishments, no matter how trivial they may seem to you. Brainstorm about what you've gained from your experiences and be sure you are able to talk about what you've accomplished. You probably have more to offer than you think!

From this growing collection of records and achievements, you will begin to get a clearer picture of what you really have to offer the world.

ORGANIZING YOUR DATA

The resume-writing process begins with the assembly and organization of all the personal, educational and employment data from which you will choose the pieces that actually end up on paper. If this information *is* properly organized, writing your resume is a relatively easy task, just shifting data from one format to another.

On the following pages, we have prepared five *Data Input Sheets* (with multiple copies of some, where needed). The first three—covering employment, education and awards/activities—are essential to any resume. The last two—covering military service and language skills—are important if, of course, they apply to you.

Here are some pointers on how to fill out these all-important Data Sheets:

Employment Data Input Sheet: You will need to record the basic information—employer's name, address and phone number, dates of employment and your supervisors name—for your own files anyway. It may be an important addition to your networking list and will be necessary should you be asked to supply a reference list.

"Duties" should be a one- or two-sentence paragraph describing what you did on this job, with particular emphasis on the skills required to accomplish set tasks. For example, if you worked as a hostess in a restaurant, your work experience section might read as follows:

"Responsible for the delivery of 250 meals at dinnertime and the supervision of 20 waiters and busboys. Coordinated reservations. Responsible for check and payment verification."

Prepare one employment data sheet for each job you have held, no matter how short the job (yes, summer jobs count) or how limited you may think it is. While we've included four blank Input Sheets for your use, you may need to prepare more.

Educational Data Input Sheet: If you're in college, omit details on high school. If you're a graduate student, list details on both graduate and undergraduate coursework. If you have not yet graduated, list your anticipated date of graduation. If more than a year away, indicate the numbers of credits earned through the most recent semester to be completed.

Awards/Activities Data Input Sheet: This is where to list your participation in the Student Government, Winter Carnival Press Committee, Math

Club, Ski Patrol, etc. Make sure you indicate if you held any positions in any clubs. Any volunteer work should also be listed on this form, as well as awards and honors from your school (prestigious high school awards can still be included here, even if you're in graduate school), community groups, church groups, clubs, etc.

Military Service Data Input Sheet: Many useful skills are learned in the armed forces. A military stint often hastens the maturation process, making you a more attractive candidate. So if you have served in the military, make sure you include details in your resume.

Language Data Input Sheet: An extremely important section for those of you with a real proficiency in a second language. And *do* make sure you have at least conversational fluency in the language(s) you list. One year of college French doesn't count, but if you've studied abroad, you probably are fluent or near-fluent. Such a talent could be invaluable, especially if you hope to work in the international arena.

CREATING YOUR FIRST RESUME

Your resume is a one- or two-page summary of you—your education, skills, employment experience and career objective(s). It is not a biography, but a "quick and dirty" way to identify and describe you to potential employers.

In order to begin preparing your resume, you will need to assemble all the following information (which should have been done in the previous section. If not, go back and try again!):

1. The name and address of your college or high school, if applicable, including expected graduation date.

2. Your grade point average and class rank. (Express the latter as the number of completed trimester or semester grades your rank includes. For example: "100/308, includes six semesters, freshman through junior year.")

3. Important classes you've taken, especially those that relate to your intended career.

4. A concise career objective.

5. Clubs, honor societies and other extracurricular activities—name of each and dates in which you participated. Be sure you include any leadership positions you held.

6. Awards and honors you have received.

7. The names, addresses and telephone numbers of all your past employers.

8. The key personnel with whom you worked and a concise summary of the work you performed.

EMPLOYMENT DATA INPUT SHEET (1)

Employer name: _____

Address: _____

Phone: _____ Dates of Employment: _____

Supervisor's Name & Title: _____

Duties: _____

_____

_____

Other Important Information: _____

_____

_____

EMPLOYMENT DATA INPUT SHEET (2)

Employer name: _____

Address: _____

Phone: _____ Dates of Employment: _____

Supervisor's Name & Title: _____

Duties: _____

_____

_____

Other Important Information: _____

_____

_____

EMPLOYMENT DATA INPUT SHEET (3)

Employer name: _____

Address: _____

Phone: _____ Dates of Employment: _____

Supervisor's Name & Title: _____

Duties: _____

_____

_____

Other Important Information: _____

_____

_____

EMPLOYMENT DATA INPUT SHEET (4)

Employer name: _____

Address: _____

Phone: _____ Dates of Employment: _____

Supervisor's Name & Title: _____

Duties: _____

_____

_____

Other Important Information: _____

_____

_____

EDUCATIONAL DATA INPUT SHEET

College/High school name: _____

Address: _____

Phone: _____ Years Attended: _____

Degrees Earned: _____ Major: _____ Minor: _____

Honors: _____

_____

Important Courses: _____

_____

_____

_____

_____

EDUCATIONAL DATA INPUT SHEET

College/High school name: _____

Address: _____

Phone: _____ Years Attended: _____

Degrees Earned: _____ Major: _____ Minor: _____

Honors: _____

_____

Important Courses: _____

_____

_____

_____

_____

AWARDS/ACTIVITIES DATA INPUT SHEET

Club: _____ Office(s) held: _____

Description of activities: _____

Club: _____ Office(s) held: _____

Description of activities: _____

Club: _____ Office(s) held: _____

Description of activities: _____

Club: _____ Office(s) held: _____

Description of activities: _____

Club: _____ Office(s) held: _____

Description of activities: _____

Volunteer work: _____

Description of activities: _____

_____

Volunteer work: _____

Description of activities: _____

_____

Volunteer work: _____

Description of activities: _____

_____

Awards/Honors: _____

_____

_____

MILITARY SERVICE DATA INPUT SHEET

Branch: _____ Rank (at Discharge):_____

Dates of Service: _____

Responsibilities: _____

_____

_____

Special Training and/or Skills: _____

_____

_____

LANGUAGE DATA INPUT SHEET (2)

Language: _____

    ❏ Read   ❏ Write   ❏ Converse

Background (number of years studied, travel, etc.): _____

_____

Language: _____

    ❏ Read   ❏ Write   ❏ Converse

Background : _____

_____

Language: _____

    ❏ Read   ❏ Write   ❏ Converse

Background : _____

_____

9. Any letters of recommendation from these employers, your teachers, counselors, etc.

10. Hobbies and other interests.

11. A list of references.

12. If you have served in the military, you should also collect pertinent service records.

There are a lot of options about what to include or leave out. In general, we suggest you always include the following data:

1. Your name, address and telephone number

2. Pertinent educational history (grades, class rank, activities, etc.)

3. Pertinent work history

4. Academic honors

5. Memberships in organizations

You have the option of including the following:

1. Your career objective

2. Personal data

3. Hobbies

4. Military service history (if applicable)

5. References

And you should *never* include the following:

1. Photographs or illustrations (of yourself or anything else, unless they are required by your profession—e.g., actors' composites)

GUIDELINES FOR RESUME PREPARATION

Your resume should be limited to a single page if possible, two at most. When you're laying out the resume, try to leave a reasonable amount of "white space"—generous margins all around and spacing between entries. It should be typed or printed (not xeroxed) on 8 1/2" x 11" white, cream or ivory stock. The ink should be black or, at most, a royal blue. Don't scrimp on the paper quality—use the best bond you can afford. And since printing 100 or even 200 copies will cost little more than 50, if you do decide to print your resume, *over*estimate your needs, and opt for the highest quantity you think you may need. Prices at various "quick print" storefronts will not break the bank; but the quality look printing affords may leave the right impression.

Using Power Words For Impact

Be brief. Use phraseology rather than complete sentences. Your resume is a summary of your talents, not an English Lit paper. Choose your words carefully and use "power words" whenever possible. "Organized" is more powerful than "put together;" "supervised" better than "oversaw;" "formulated" better than "thought up." Strong words like these can make the most mundane clerical work sound like a series of responsible, professional positions. And, of course, they will tend to make your resume stand out. Here's a "starter list" of words that you may want to use in your resume:

achieved	administered	advised
analyzed	applied	arranged
budgeted	calculated	classified
communicated	completed	computed
conceptualized	coordinated	critiqued
delegated	determined	developed
devised	directed	established
evaluated	executed	formulated
gathered	generated	guided
implemented	improved	initiated
instituted	instructed	introduced
invented	issued	launched
lectured	litigated	lobbied
managed	negotiated	operated
organized	overhauled	planned
prepared	presented	presided
programmed	promoted	recommended
researched	reviewed	revised
reorganized	regulated	selected
solved	scheduled	supervised
systematized	taught	tested
traced	trained	updated
utilized	wrote	

Choosing A Format

There is not a lot of mystery here—your background will generally lead you to the right format. For an entry-level job applicant with limited work experience, the **chronological** format, which organizes your educational and employment history by date (most recent first) is the obvious choice. For older or more-experienced applicants, either the **functional**—which emphasizes the duties and responsibilities of all your jobs over the course of your career—or **combination**—half-way between chronological and functional—may be more suitable. While I have tended to emphasize the chronological format in this chapter, one of the other two may well be the right one for you. The next chapter contains many examples of all three varieties.

REACHING FOR YOUR STAR

Two vitally important parts of your resume will be the Objective and Summary of Qualifications sections, which will set the tone for the entire document. Basically they are an attempt to inform the reader of the kind of job you are looking for and why you are qualified to do it.

Yes, it's finally time to tell everyone what you really want to be when you grow up!

Creating A Concise Career Objective

If you did the job description research detailed in chapter 3, composing a concise, narrowly-targeted objective should be easy—just describe the job you're looking for. Rather than trying to describe this process in more detail, I think some concrete examples will make it clear. So I've drafted five Objectives based upon some of the job descriptions we reviewed in chapter 3. (Note: Some of the resulting objectives are probably *overly* specific, because they were based on very specific job descriptions.):

JOB TITLE	SAMPLE OBJECTIVE
Property Manager	Seeking a position in multi-unit residence management where I can best utilize my experience in building maintenance, debt collection, services coordination and selling new rentals.
Sales Trainee	A structured position in outside sales requiring well-developed communications, administrative and telemarketing skills.
Advertising Account Trainee	A position in which research, budget-planning and people skills can be utilized to in an agency environment.
Reporter	Seek challenging reportorial position with major newspaper or wire service
Inventory Control Clerk	Seek position that will utilize my data entry skills and systems techniques in management of Kardex and computer inventory systems.

Summarizing Your Qualifications

Some counselors prefer than only those of you with extensive work experience include a "Summary of Qualifications" section; in fact, many of these same counselors aren't in favor of Objectives on entry-level resumes, either.

I disagree on both counts. While there may be valid reasons to consider such a section optional (at worst), such supporting data clearly illustrates why and how you are qualified for the career objective you've described. It's like the claim that your new car can hit 150 mph (your Objective). By noting the details of the specially-constructed engine (the Summary of Qualifications), you have concisely supported your initial claim.

I'll leave the decision to you, but if your education has been highly focused, enabling you to document extensive and intensive coursework in an applicable area, or have specific (if limited) experience that perfectly matches your Objective, I'd include such a section.

To illustrate, consider the case of a graduate student seeking an entry-level position in marketing research. The Objective might read:

"A position in marketing, with emphasis on research, planning and concept development, for a product-oriented company."

The matching qualifications statement might read:

"Intensive coursework in business administration, including statistical methodology, market research, management, strategic planning and new product development, plus 25 graduate-level credits in accounting and business law. Summer internship in the Marketing Department of CBS Records Division."

REFERENCES & LETTERS OF RECOMMENDATION

When you request letters of recommendation from teachers, professors, counselors, coaches or friends, give them a copy of your resume. Not only will that make their task easier, but you'll probably get a clearer and more detailed recommendation from them.

If you receive permission from past employers, professors, etc. to list them as references, make sure you include their name, title, company and phone number. You may wish to prepare an extensive list of references from which more concise lists can be extracted, depending on the particular job or company involved. Advice varies on whether or not to include your list of references with your resume. I personally counsel against it. A list of pertinent references can easily be sent along (or handed to) an interested employer...after he or she has confirmed that interest by asking for it.

TWO SPECIAL CASES

Two special situations need to be noted for those of you to whom they apply:

1). If you are a returning serviceman, your military history should take precedence—position it immediately after your Objective and before any other educational or experience listings.

2). If you have any sort of physical handicap, feel free to note it in your cover letters or, if you prefer, mention it in discussions prior to your interview, but it's unnecessary to include such details in your resume. Unless your limitation will put you at a disadvantage in a particular work situation (machinery handling) or requires special access equipment to facilitate your movement at the workplace (ramps), don't make anything of it.

We have prepared a fill-in-the-blanks resume form on the following pages that will allow you to create an effective resume within minutes. This is no time to be humble! List everything you've done, even if it seems trivial to you. It's also not the time to exaggerate! Be truthful!

An important suggestion: When you've completed writing and designing your resume, have a couple of close friends or family members proofread it for typographical errors *before* you type it or send it to the printer. A fresh look from someone not as familiar with it as you will catch these glaring (and potentially embarrassing) errors before they're duplicated a hundred times.

A MANY-SPLENDORED THING

Though the focus of all our discussions so far has been on seeking and getting the job you want, remember that your resume is a flexible document. There are many other uses for it. Here are three key ways your resume can help you:

• **Preparing for college**—It's the best organizing tool available. Having your completed resume handy (and having gone through the exercises necessary to prepare it) will be invaluable as you start to fill out applications and consider essay topics.

• **At the bank**—If you need to apply for a college loan, supplying a professional-looking resume along with the required financial statement will make a good impression. Since such background information is important to their decision-making process, you're actually making the loan officer's job easier. They appreciate that.

• **Starting your own business**—If you're fearless and absolutely convinced you can construct a better mousetrap, you may well decide to go around the job search process and just create your own job—by starting your own business. As you set up shop, you will need to raise capital, purchase machinery and equipment, establish credit, introduce yourself to potential clients—let your resume speak for you...and eloquently.

FILL-IN-THE-BLANKS RESUME OUTLINE

Name : _____

Address : _____

City, state, zip code : _____

Telephone number : _____

• OBJECTIVE : _____

_____

_____

• EDUCATION:

School name : _____

Address : _____

Expected graduation date : _____Grade point average : _____

Class rank : _____

Important classes you have taken, especially those that relate to your intended career:

_____

_____

_____

_____

_____

• EXTRACURRICULAR ACTIVITIES (Activity name and dates participated):

_____

_____

_____

_____

_____

• AWARDS AND HONORS (Award name, date received and the significance of the award. Example: Wilson Pickering Scholarship, 1987, awarded to senior student at Peabody High School with superior academic achievements and an expressed interest in pursuing higher education in the natural sciences.):

_____

_____

_____

• WORK EXPERIENCE (Job title, name of business, business address, dates of employment and your major responsibilities. Include volunteer experience in this category. List your experiences with the *most recent dates first!):*

_____

_____

_____

_____

_____

_____

• INTERESTS AND HOBBIES:

_____

_____

_____

_____

_____

• REFERENCES (A list of at least three names with their titles, addresses and telephone numbers. Before you include anyone on this list, talk with them and make sure you have their permission to use their name as a reference. You should also ask them what they are willing to say about you to a potential employer. You may want to list the same people from whom you request letters of recommendation.):

1. _____

_____

_____

2. _____

_____

_____

3. _____

_____

_____

4. _____

_____

TO THINE OWN SELF BE TRUE

Unless you have some unusual limitation I don't know about, each of you should be perfectly capable of preparing your own resume...especially if you follow all the advice in this book. So avoid the trap of having some "professional" write it for you. Get help and assistance wherever you feel you need to, but make sure your resume is in your own words—interviewers are particularly adept at ferreting out so-called "professionally-prepared" ones. You will not be commended for having one—at best, it says you're just lazy; at worst, it seriously calls into question your mastery of even basic communications skills.

Chapter 7 offers help of the best kind—a diversified inventory of actual resumes. Look through all of them. Note the various styles and formats. Seek out the tone or style that approximates your own.

Seeing is believing—you can do it, too!

CHAPTER SEVEN

Try Before You Buy

This chapter contains 25 sample resumes taken from real life. Its purpose is to give you concrete examples of how other people in similar circumstances have styled their resumes. We have included samples covering a broad array of professions and experience levels.

The following guide will help you locate those resumes most pertinent to your own situation:

I have sprinkled various formats, styles and typefaces (typewritten and typset) throughout, so whatever your situation, you should look over all the samples.

What if a sample resume for the particular job you're looking for isn't included? Since I've only included 25 samples, the odds are it *won't* be. But it shouldn't be hard to adapt one of the samples to your particular needs, since they cover *in general* all the possibilities. In most cases, merely tailoring the "Objective" to your own circumstances and replacing information in the other sections with your own educational and work experience would result in a superior resume.

A MATTER OF STYLE?

The style and format you will use in your own resume is really more a question of emphasis than anything else. The **chronological** and **functional** resume formats can be used almost interchangeably, though for most students the chronological is preferred.

Unless you have a long list of skills, it is usually preferable to highlight your educational background. But if your skills inventory is exceptionally broad and varied, you will want to highlight it—even if your work experience is very limited. In this circumstance, the functional format would probably work best.

The **combination** resume format is best used when there is considerable work experience.

The traditional sequencing of sections for the three types of resume formats follows:

Chronological:

Contact information
Objective
Qualifications (OPTIONAL)
Education
Work experience

Functional:

Contact information
Objective
Qualifications (OPTIONAL)
Skills/achievements
Education

Combination:

Contact information
Objective
Qualifications (OPTIONAL)
Skills/achievements
Work experience
Education

CHRONOLOGICAL RESUME — SALES

GAIL S. POPPER
127 West Allen Street
Washington, D.C. 20030
202/473-1852

OBJECTIVE: A professional sales position, leading to management, in information processing, where administrative and technical experience, initiative and interpersonal skills can be utilized to maximize sales and promote good customer relations.

EDUCATION: B.A. in Communication, 1983.
George Mason University, Fairfax, Virginia.

- Courses in interpersonal communication, psychology and public speaking.

- Worked full-time, earning 100% of educational and personal experiences.

TECHNICAL EXPERIENCE: MCT Corporation (Washington, D.C.)
Office management and materials production responsibilities. Planned and reorganized word processing center. Initiated time and cost studies, which saved company $30,000 in additional labor costs. Improved efficiency of personnel. 1986 to present.

TECHNICAL SKILLS: Five years of experience in operating Mag card and high speed printers: IBM 6240, Mag A, I, II, IBM 6640, and Savin word processor.

SALES EXPERIENCE: Sears Roebuck & Co.,(Washington, D.C.)
Promoted improved community relations with company. Solved customer complaints. Reorganized product displays. Handled orders. 1983 - 1985.

References Available Upon Request

FUNCTIONAL RESUME — SALES

GAIL S. POPPER
127 West Allen Street
Washington, D.C. 20030
202/473-1852

OBJECTIVE: A professional sales position, leading to management, in information processing, where administrative and technical experience, initiative and interpersonal skills can be utilized to maximize sales and promote good customer relations.

SALES/ CUSTOMER RELATIONS: Promoted improved community relations with business. Solved customer complaints. Recruited new clients. Reorganized product displays. Maintained inventory. Received and filled orders.

PLANNING/ ORGANIZING: Planned and re-organized word processing center. Initiated time and cost studies, which saved company additional labor costs and improved efficiency of personnel. Developed and organized technical reference room for more effective utilization of equipment. Created new tracking and filing system for Mag cards which resulted in eliminating redundancy and improving turnaround time.

TECHNICAL: Five years of experience in operating Mag card and high speed printers: IBM 6240, Mag A, I, II, IBM 6640, and Savin word processor.

EDUCATION: B.A. in Communication, 1983.
George Mason University, Fairfax, Virginia.

  • Courses in interpersonal communication, psychology, and public speaking.

  • Worked full-time in earning 100% of educational and personal expenses.

PERSONAL: Excellent health ... enjoy challenges ... interested in productivity ... willing to relocate and travel.

REFERENCES: Available upon request.

COMBINATION RESUME — SALES

GAIL S. POPPER
127 West Allen Street
Washington, D.C. 20030
202/473-1852

OBJECTIVE: A professional sales position, leading to management, in information processing, where administrative and technical experience, initiative and interpersonal skills can be utilized to maximize sales and promote good customer relations.

SALES/ CUSTOMER RELATIONS: Promoted improved community relations with business. Solved customer complaints. Recruited new clients. Re-organized product displays. Maintained inventory. Received and filled orders.

PLANNING/ ORGANIZING: Planned and re-organized word processing center. Initiated time and cost studies, which saved company $30,000 in additional labor costs and improved efficiency of personnel. Developed and organized technical reference room for more effective utilization Of equipment. Created new tracking and filing system for Mag cards which resulted in eliminating redundancy and improving turnaround time.

TECHNICAL: Five years of experience in operating Mag card and high speed printers: IBM 6240, Mag A, I, II, IBM 6640, and Savin word processor.

EMPLOYMENT EXPERIENCE: MCT Corporation, Washington, D.C.
Martin Computer Services, Annandale, Virginia.

EDUCATION: B.A. in Communication, 1983.
George Mason University, Fairfax, Virginia.

- Courses in interpersonal communication, psychology, and public speaking.
- Worked full-time in earning 100% of educational and personal expenses.

PERSONAL: Excellent health ... enjoy challenges ... interested in productivity ... willing to relocate and travel.

REFERENCES: Available upon request

AIRLINE RESERVATIONS CLERK

Mary Fulsom
68 West Turnpike
Kalamazoo; Michigan 68678
(614) 383-8989

JOB
OBJECTIVE: A position as an airline reservations clerk.for
                 a national or regional carrier.

EDUCATION:

December 1987   Graduated from Laverne Bell Modeling School,
                     Chicago, Il.

June 1987   Commercial Diploma
                     Mother Seton High School, Chicago, Il.

EXPERIENCE:

1987-Present   <u>Reservationist Trainee</u> Great North Airlines,
                 Detroit, Mi. (while completing modeling courses)

                 • Make reservations for GN Airlines on all
                   routes flown (primarily Michigan and
                   Wisconsin)
                 • Arrange connecting flights
                 • Utilize Teletype
                 • Enter flight/ticketing information.
                 • Employee of the Month four times in one
                   year.

CASHIER

ROBERTA CALDWELL
47 London Way
Cromwell, New Jersey 07861
201-199-8234

OBJECTIVE   A full-time cashier position in a large retail store, preferably in a shopping center in Cromwell vicinity.

EXPERIENCE

1985-1987   Cashier, part-time, Bergen Supermarket, Bergen, N.J.
Worked 20 hours a week as cashier at checkout counter.

1985-1987 (Summers)   Assistant Bookkeeper and Cashier, Howard's Retail Store, Cromwell, N.J.
Collected and recorded mail-order payments as well as those made in person at credit office; prepared monthly statement; assisted bookkeeper in all record-keeping.

1984-1985   Accounts Receivable Clerk, Homowak Mart, New Bergen,N.J. (part-time)
Received payments made in credit office and by mail, recorded cash, issued receipts. Prepared monthly statements to customers.

EDUCATION

1987   Completed six-month course in Business Machines at Cromwell Business School.

1984-1987   Attended Cromwell High School. Completed requirements for Commercial Diploma.

INTERESTS

Gourmet cooking, sewing, pen-and-ink drawing.

REFERENCES

Furnished upon request.

RETURNING SERVICEMAN

THOMAS JONES
607 North Lakeland Drive
Memphis, Tennessee 21756
(615) 457-0202

JOB OBJECTIVE

To secure a management trainee position with a large consumer-products company

MILITARY SERVICE

June, 1983 to June, 1987

U.S. Navy Apprentice Seaman promoted to Seaman 1st Class
Stationed in Alaska
Honorably discharged

BUSINESS EXPERIENCE

August, 1981 to May, 1983

Management Trainee - W.T. Grant, Nashville, Tennessee

Duties included waiting on customers in every department of the store, operating the cash registers, assisting in the stock room and keeping track of merchandise in stock.

EDUCATION

1971 - 1976

Nashville Commercial High School, Nashville, Tennessee

HOBBIES

Bowling, Swimming, Camping

REFERENCES

Available on request

HIGH SCHOOL TO COLLEGE

GILDA H. PLEASANT
80 Outer Freeway
Dallas, TX 87540
(214) 887-0782

OBJECTIVE

Acceptance to a Midwest liberal arts college with a superior program in English literature.

EDUCATION

Graduating in June, 1988, from Dethis High School (521 Fifth St., Dallas, TX 87521). College prep core curriculum including honors English 11 and 12.

GPA 3.2 (A = 4.0); Class rank: 48/502.

EXTRACURRICULAR ACTIVITIES

Writers Club (President-1986 & 1987); Yearbook staff (Editor-1987-88); Field hockey (4 years); Cheer squad (3 years); United Way.

HONORS & AWARDS

National Honor Society, Senior Class President.

WORK EXPERIENCE

1985 & 1986 (summers) Kiach Publishing Co., (832 Dallas Pike, Dallas, TX 87440). Intern in editorial department. Duties included reading manuscripts, typing editor's reports, filing.

1986 & 1987 (school year) Simmons Public Library (851 5th Ave., Simmons, TX 87550). Library assistant. Duties included cataloguing, typing and filing.

HOBBIES

Reading, writing, sports

REFERENCES

Available upon request

HIGH SCHOOL TO COLLEGE

JOHN F. FERRADAY
221 Boylston Street
Bronx, N.Y. 10128
(212) 585-8585

OBJECTIVE: Matriculation at a Liberal Arts college to pursue a course of study in computer science.

EDUCATION: June 1987 Graduate, Franklin H.S., Bronx, N.Y. 10128
Academic degree. GPA 2.9
Class rank, 127/322

ACTIVITIES: Math Club (Secretary), Varsity Football, Community Relations Board, Member of Student Council

AWARDS: Math Cup Sigma Cup (Honors)

WORK
EXPERIENCE: 1985-86 (summers): Counterman, Red Lobster Drive-in. Cabrini Boulevard, Bronx, N.Y. 10128

Christmas, 1985-86: Stock Room Clerk, R.H. Macy & Co. Parkchester, N.Y. 10128

PERSONAL: Hobbies: swimming, hiking, camping. Red Cross Life Savers Accredited.

REFERENCES: Available upon request

HIGH SCHOOL TO JUNIOR COLLEGE

Mary Marshall
West Broadway
Gouvenor, N.Y. 10011
(914) 827-2398

OBJECTIVE

Acceptance at a Junior College offering a business and accounting major

EDUCATION

June 1987 commercial graduate, County H.S., Canton, N.Y. 16011
GPA 3.2. Class rank - 115/329

ACTIVITIES

Student Govt. typing pool, Girl's ski team, Pep Squad

AWARDS

Varsity C. Club

WORK EXPERIENCE

Clerk-typist, Alvira Insurance, Main Street, Canton, N.Y. 16011
Part-time, 1986.

INTERESTS

All outdoor sports plus cross-country skiing. Fund-raising activities for
Salvation Army.

SKILLS

Typing: 60 wpm. Shorthand: 75 wpm

REFERENCES

Furnished upon request

HIGH SCHOOL TO TRADE SCHOOL

Shawn Clark
101 St. Mark's Place
Brooklyn, N.Y. 10780
(718) 828-0091

OBJECTIVE: Acceptance at a Trade School offering certification in electronics and TV repair

EDUCATION: June 1987 Graduate Boys High School, Brooklyn, N.Y. 10483 GPA 2.7, Class rank 220/490. Commercial course.

ACTIVITIES: Arts & Crafts Council (President); TV Studio Club (Manager)

AWARDS: H.S. Emmy's, Chief Stage Hand/Electrician Gold Prize, set design, 1986

WORK EXPERIENCE: Rockland Auto Radio, Assistant Mechanic; summers 1983-86, after school (20 hrs./week) 1984-86

PERSONAL: Build model airplanes and electronically operated small sailing boats.

REFERENCES: Available upon request

ACCOUNTANT

DOREEN L. FERNANDEZ
11541 North Stebbens Avenue
Englewood, New Jersey 09876
(201) 445-5867

OBJECTIVE: Junior accountant position in a public accounting firm

EDUCATION: Bachelor of Science, Montclair State College, Montclair, New Jersey, 1987. Major: Accounting (CPA emphasis); Minor: Computer Science. GPA: 3.62 (A = 4.00).

Representative accounting courses included:

- Current Issues in Financial Accounting
- Computer Based Information Systems
- Advanced Tax Law
- Seminar for Public Accounting

Representative computer science courses included:

- Computer Simulation and Modeling
- Data Processing Systems
- Data Base Management Systems

RELATED
EXPERIENCE: Business manager of Montclair Monitor, undergraduate newspaper (1985-1987)

Class treasurer for all four years of college

Professional accounting participation, included three years in Accounting Club (two years as treasurer).

WORK
EXPERIENCE: Assistant Manager, Lucky Stores, Englewood Cliffs, N. J.

Responsible for all facets of produce management including inventory control, quality assurance, scheduling of hours, and supervision of personnel.

REFERENCES: Available upon request.

DIETICIAN

Rose Greco
2109 Park Avenue
New York, N.Y. 10028
(212) 887-0280

JOB OBJECTIVE:

Position with food processing company as a staff specialist.

EDUCATION:

Nutrition Major. B.S. degree, Michigan State University, 1986. Graduate courses on Environmental Effect on Man and His Menu, Special Food for the Elderly, and Food Chemistry.

These courses provided an excellent background in elements of nutrition as related to ecology, problems of the elderly, and commercial food processing.

HONORS:

Dean's List throughout four years of college.

EXPERIENCE:

Summers/1985-87: Purdey State Hospital, Detroit, MI.

Assistant to Chief Dietician: Helped translate convalescent diets into actual meals; selected and delivered special meals to diet patients.

School year/1985-1987: Michigan State Student Cafeteria

Assistant Nutritionist: Worked with Chief Nutritionist and her staff of 18 to plan over 300 menus per year. Responsible for scheduling waiters and all temporary help.

DRAFTSMAN

DENISE BROWN
3522 Alhameda Blvd., #10
Tucson, Arizona
(602) 488-8162

OBJECTIVE

A position utilizing my drafting, graphics, light machine and computer skills.

SKILLS

o Complete computer literacy—experienced in a variety of spreadsheet and word processing programs.

o Two years of precision drafting in mechanical and electronic drawing.

o Office management—filing, reception and document authorization.

o Ability to create structured information letters for special purpose business communications.

o Graphic arts skills applicable to high quality silk screen projects, film development and offset press operations.

EDUCATION

Currently attending Mesa Community College, Mesa, Arizona.

Major courses in area of concentration: Business Communications, Business Mathematics, Word/Information Processing, Automation, Mechanical and Electronic Drafting.

Other important coursework: Office Support, Graphic Arts, Mechanical Drafting, Personal Computer Lab. Word processing, Rockwell Act-Drafting Techniques.

WORK EXPERIENCE

Summer 1987: Machinist Aid, Arrow Swiss, Phoenix, Arizona 92804.

Worked under the direction of owner, manufacturing small parts requiring precision drill press and lathe operations.

1984 to 1987: Babysitting

Responsible for the well being and safety of children in their home. Managed household activities which include feeding, bathing, disciplinary actions, and overnight responsibilities.

SPECIAL INTERESTS

Computers—familiar with IBM/PC, Macintosh, Apple IIE, and Commodore.

REFERENCES

Will be furnished upon request.

HOUSEKEEPER/DIETICIAN

Coralee Land
101 South 12th Street
Philadelphia, Pa. 19123
(215) 886-1397

OBJECTIVE: Position requiring supervisory ability as housekeeper/ dietician in resort hotel or motel.

EDUCATION: B.S. Cornell University, Ithaca, N.Y. 1987.

Major: Home Economics
Minor: English
GPA 3.3 (A = 4.0); Class rank 189/854

ACTIVITIES: Home Economics Club, 1983-86 (President, 1985 & 1986)
Nutrition Society of America (Chairperson, New York Region, 1986-87)

EXPERIENCE: <u>Assistant Dietician</u> Henry Hudson Hotel, Port Jervis, N.Y.

Responsible for planning menus; functioned as hostess and supervised 5 waiters and 4 busboys.

REFERENCES: Available upon request.

JUNIOR PRODUCT MANAGER

JIM BEAM
76 Cortlandt St.,
New York, NY 10017
(212)555-1111

Career Objective: A position as a junior product manager at a consumer goods product company.

SUMMARY

I am completing my degree in journalism, specializing in marketing, at University State. Last summer, I interned as an assistant account executive (with copywriting responsibilities) for a local advertising agency. I also have one year's experience selling advertising space (and supervising a staff of three salespeople) on my college newspaper. Both jobs have convinced me I will be successful in brand/product management work.

EXPERIENCE

Summer, 1985 & 86: Intern, Kay Silver & Associates, Inc.
Summer, 1984 : Intern, Committee to Re-elect Kim Kerr

1985/86 school year:Ad Director, *The Daily Planet*
1986/87 school year:Salesman, Joe's University Book Store.

EDUCATION

B.A. Journalism (Marketing) University State - June, 1987
(summa cum laude).

PROFESSIONAL MEMBERSHIPS AND BUSINESS SKILLS

Member of the young Professionals Division of the Advertising Club of New York and the American Marketing Association (student chapter at University State. Skills: Sales, media placement, typing (50 wpm), computer literate.

PERSONAL

Age: 21: Health: Excellent: Fluent (read/write/speak) in German and French.

References Available Upon Request

RESEARCHER (PUBLISHING)

Joan Jamel
220 Broadway Avenue
Easton, Pa. 16917
(814) 099-6145

OBJECTIVE: Utilize research and administrative skills to provide background material for feature writers at a major newspaper or magazine publishing company.

EDUCATION: Pennsylvania State University, B.A. June, 1986

- Major: English (Writing Option)
  Minor: Journalism and Philosophy
- GPA 3.7; Class rank, 189/2,107
- Head of research for school paper 1984-1986.
- Played three varsity sports for four years—All-American 2nd team, soccer, 1986.

EXPERIENCE:
1985-86   WRSC Radio. State College, PA. (25 hrs./week)

- Gathered, wrote and produced news; responsible for writing and producing shows on State College athletes and coaches, both men and women.
- Organized and developed community-oriented program on "Women's Equality Day;" responsible for researching and writing various radio spots, Bicentennial Minutes and Sports Quiz questions.

1983-1985   The Easton Times-Herald, Easton, PA (Summers)

- Assisted head of Research Department.
- Responsible for updating library resources.
- Worked with a variety of reporters and freelance feature writers, providing background and detailed information where required.

SOCIAL WORKER

Adrienne Delafield
47 Oak Tree Street
Crescent City, Missouri 60116
(816) 529-1199

OBJECTIVE

Children's Caseworker in Public or Private Hospital

EDUCATION

B.S. Social Work, Southern Missouri State College, Springfield, Missouri, 1986. Concentrated training in social work with an emphasis on psychiatric and pediatric care.

WORK EXPERIENCE

Family Caseworker, Kansas City State Hospital, 1987.

Interviewed members of families at the hospital or at their homes to help them adjust to social/economic problems. Proposed plans for assisting patients.

PROFESSIONAL AFFILIATIONS

National Association of Social Workers
National Caseworkers Association

CIVIL ENGINEER

PATRICK E. CARLYSLE
2176 Delmar Avenue, #4823
Peoria, Illinois 60616
(312) 546-8600

OBJECTIVE: An entry-level position offering an opportunity for growth in the civil engineering field.

EDUCATION: Illinois Institute of Technology, Bachelor of Science in Civil Engineering

Major GPA; 3.58/4.00; Overall GPA: 3.48/4.00

COURSE WORK:

In Major (Semester Hrs)	Supporting Courses
Strength of Materials (4)	Mathematics (17)
Fluid Mechanics (4)	Physics (11)
Structural Analysis (3)	Chemistry (15)
Reinforced Concrete (4)	Geology (5)
Transportation Engineering (3)	English (9)
Pavement Design (3)	French (7)
Soil Mechanics (4)	Sociology (3)
Advanced Soil Mechanics (3)	Economics (7)
Structural Steel Design (4)	Humanities (9)
Prestressed Concrete (3)	Psychology (3)
Foundational Engineering (3)	
Surveying (4)	

RESEARCH EXPERIENCE: Dr. James Whitney, Professor in Structural Design
Illinois Institute of Technology, Fall, 1986

• Statics Problem: Performed solutions for a new statics book. Worked on more than 100 problems.

• Concrete Beam: Worked on computer program dealing with analysis and design of concrete beams.

Patrick E. Carlysle -2-

RESEARCH
EXPERIENCE
(Continued):   Dr. Floyd Davis, Assistant Professor in Civil Engineering
                  Illinois Institute of Technology, Spring, 1987

                  • Seepage Problem: Worked on a computer program
                  dealing with two dimensional seepage under a sheet
                  piling.

                  • Embankment Loading: Working on a computer program
                  that will be used to determine the stress distribution
                  under an embankment loading.

HONORS &
ACTIVITIES: Dean's List, Fall 1986
                  Chi Epsilon, Civil Engineering Honor Society (Member)
                  International Students Advisory Board (Member)
                  American Society of Civil Engineers (Assoc. Member)

REFERENCES: Available upon request

PETROLEUM ENGINEER

STEPHEN STEVENS

Permanent Address: Temporary Address:
2201 West 105th Street   119 Clark Ave.,#9
Waco, Texas 78712   Austin, Texas 78717
(512) 277-2081   (512) 265-7666

PROFESSIONAL OBJECTIVE

To obtain an entry-level position in the operational areas of petroleum engineering at a major oil company.

EDUCATION

THE UNIVERSITY OF TEXAS AT AUSTIN

Baccalaureate Degree Candidate in Petroleum Engineering. Degree expected May, 1987.

ACADEMIC PROFILE

Completed Courses:

- Reservoir Engineering
- Applied Reservoir Eng.
- Applied Reservoir Analysis
- Reservoir Modeling
- Engineering Secondary Recovery
- Well Treating and Evaluation
- Rock and Fluid Lab.
- Oil Well Drilling
- Drilling Design & Production
- Petroleum Engineering Design
- Formation Evaluation

WORK EXPERIENCE

SUPERVISOR — SEARS WAREHOUSE, Austin, Texas (Part-time summer employment) 1985 & 1986.

- Supervised five warehouse employees during the night shift.

ASST. DEPARTMENT MANAGER — K MART- Austin, Texas (Part-time during school year; approx. 20 hours/week) 1984 & 1985

- Responsible for overall maintenance as well as scheduling and supervision of four part-time employees in the housewares department.
- Revised merchandise layout and recommended changes that resulted in increased product visibility.

LAB ASSISTANT — UNIVERSITY OF TEXAS, Austin, Texas (Part-Time during school year; approx. 25 hours/week). 1986 & 1987

- Worked in the Instrumentation Lab and assisted in the development of a Phase Comparator system for the study of plasma physics.
- Designed an active bandpass filter circuit with predictable phase response.

ACTIVITIES/ACCOMPLISHMENTS

- Member of the Society of Petroleum Engineers
- Member of the Engineering Club
- Working knowledge of INTERACT, CMS, and IBM PC computers

ELECTRICAL ENGINEER

ELI JASON
1500 Dunes Circle
Crescent City, California 95850
(209) 847-1026

OBJECTIVE: A technical position which utilizes my educational and technical
                background in Electrical Engineering and mathematics.

EDUCATION: University of California, Davis
                B.S. Electrical Engineering expected June 1987. GPA 3.5

                Electrical Engineering course work: Basic Electrical and Electronic
                Circuits; Circuit Theories I & II; Circuit Analysis Laboratory; Electronics I
                & II and corresponding laboratory work; Feedback Control Systems.

                System Science course work: Stochastic Processes; Probability; Statistics
                I & II; Applied Numerical Computing; Linear Programming.

                Mathematics course work: Real Analysis I & II; Fourier and Laplace
                Transfers; Linear Algebra; Mathematical Modeling.

EXPERIENCE: Lockheed Missiles and Space Company (Summer 1986)

                Worked with the statistics and parts engineering groups on various
                assignments relating to the long term degradation of stored Trident 1
                missile parts. Work included trend analyses, warehouse inspections, and
                programming in DPL.

SKILLS: Programming experience with Pascal and DPL. Have used the Unix,
                Sylbur, and Executive Operating Systems on various mainframes. Have
                had experience with the WordStar operating system on the IBM PC. Have
                also had SPICE in analyzing electronic circuits.

ACTIVITIES: Member, Circuits and Systems Society
                President, Sigma Nu Fraternity

REFERENCES: Available upon request.

CLERK-TYPIST
(Returnee To Work Force)

EVELYN PLUMER
259 Highway Lane
Danbury, CT 06810
203-555-1234

OBJECTIVE:

To provide top-quality, conscientious service as typist and office clerk in a New York City industrial firm.

EXPERIENCE

1971-1974

Typist, File Clerk

Feinberg Associates, Danbury, Connecticut.

Assembled data from legal reports, typed revisions and legal contracts, served as relief receptionist, maintained files and provided general office assistance.

1968-1971

Typist-Receptionist

Manzo Realtors, Forest Hills, New York.

Served as receptionist to large Real Estate company: typed documents related to sale and purchase of property; filed records of clients and construction companies; maintained appointment schedules.

EDUCATION

Graduated with commercial diploma from Danbury High School, June, 1968.

OFFICE SKILLS

Typing - 75 wpm; shorthand - 100 wpm; filing; calculators; dictaphone; duplicating machines; call directors.

HOBBIES

Water Skiing, Golf, Table Tennis

REFERENCES

Will be provided upon request

NIGHT SCHOOL STUDENT

RONALD W. WATSON
18828 West Highway
Seattle, Washington, 98105
(206) 465-9688

OBJECTIVE: Position as electronics technician that will utilize technical and supervisory skills developed through military service and part-time employment.

WORK
EXPERIENCE:

1985-Present   BOEING AEROSPACE, Seattle, Washington

Special Project Mechanic

• Worked on three projects simultaneously: AWACS, Air Launch Cruise Missile and Minuteman Missile.

• Installed sensitive electronic communication equipment

• Assembled the sub-assemblies

• Assembled and installed various associated components.

MILITARY
EXPERIENCE:

1975-1985   UNITED STATES NAVY

Weapons Technician, E-5 (Petty Officer)

• In charge of guidance and control test section

• Responsible for preventive and corrective maintenance on nuclear weapons systems and components.

• Maintained necessary records

• Ordered parts, tools and supplies

• Inventoried components and test equipment

• Supervised personnel

- Operated launchers.

- Served as member of damage control party, firefighting party and NBC defense team.

- Collateral duties included Naval Courier and explosives driver.

- Evaluated as being "an effective, reliable, and meticulous technician ... his troubleshooting techniques are superb (and) his behavior above reproach." Received letters of commendation for outstanding performance.

EDUCATION/
TRAINING

UNIVERSITY OF WASHINGTON

- Currently working toward B.S. Degree in Electrical Engineering Degree expected June, 1989

UNIVERSITY OF MARYLAND, Far East Division
English and Science (48 units)

REFERENCES: Available upon request

INVENTORY CLERK
(Returnee To Work Force)

REBECCA SPACE
950 Westway Road
Cheyenne, Wyoming 82007
(307) 366-2892

JOB
OBJECTIVE: Senior Clerk position requiring inventory
               control and supervisory experience.

PROFESSIONAL
EXPERIENCE:

1973-1976   **Inventory Control Clerk**
               Plymouth-Sperry Corporation

               Entered data on a Kardex system and on the
               computer. Assisted buyers by tabulating
               marketing and production control's monthly
               needs and comparing with stock to deter-
               mine order amount.

1971-1973   **Allocation Clerk**
               Larson Electronics

               Responsible for overseeing the alloca-
               tion system. Worked with purchasing
               personnel as well as receiving inspectors,
               material planners and expeditors.

1970-1971   **Inventory Bookkeeper**
               Red Owl Supermarket warehouse

               Kept records on various items and
               replenished as needed. Checked arriving
               merchandise for quantity and cost.

EDUCATION:

               Working toward an associate of arts degree
               in Business Management at Laramie Country
               Community College, Cheyenne, Wyoming.
               Expect to graduate June, 1989.

               Graduated Cheyenne High School, 1970

REFERENCES: Will be furnished upon request.

PUBLICATIONS CLERK
(Seeking Part-Time Position)

John Hamtrack
888 Wanapolis Street
New York, N.Y. 10035
212 922-8812 (home)
212 879-5500 (business)

OBJECTIVE: To utilize administrative skills as a
                  publications support clerk (part-time)

EDUCATION: Pratt Institute. B.F.A., 1987

PROFESSIONAL
EXPERIENCE:

1987—Present   Assistant Publications Clerk (part-time)
                  The Metropolitan Museum of Art, New York, N.Y.

                  Knowledge of all aspects of production and
                  composition of internal museum publications.
                  Responsibilities include photography, reduction,
                  layout, sizing and printing.

1986-87   Clerk and Assistant Bookkeeper (part-time)
                  Basic Books, Co.,New York, N.Y.

                  Supervised royalty allotments to educational
                  publications' authors, including company as well
                  as author dividends. Helped develop a computeri-
                  zation layout and feed-in to replace manual
                  system.

SKILLS: Typing (50 wpm); operation of all office
                  machines; layout and graphic skills, including
                  computer graphics, keylining and mechanical
                  preparation; photography; simple bookkeeping.

CAMP COUNSELOR
(Summer Position)

Delmor Hershkovitz
185 Spruce Street
Concord; Mass. 02189
(617) 982-2286

OBJECTIVE: To secure a position for the summer of 1988 as an athletic or senior counselor

QUALIFICATIONS: Full Red Cross training.

Life Saving Certificate, Class IV

CPR Certification

Seven letters in various high school sports

EDUCATION: Junior at University of Pennsylvania, majoring in Political Science.

EXPERIENCE: <u>Athletic Counselor</u>. Camp Win-A-Poo, Elmira, N.Y., summers 1986 and 1987 (camp closed for 1988)

• Responsible for all sports for the 12- to 16-year old age group—sports included swimming, tennis, archery and riding

• Supervised four junior counselors

• Worked under Chief Counselor—responsible for all sports and activities scheduling.

CHAPTER EIGHT ✐

Thanks And No Thanks

If you look through the card files in your local library, you'll find a surprising number of collections of letters—between literary figures, political leaders, philosophers, theologians, etc. And, of course, the intimate letters from husband to wife, lover to lover, friend to friend.

In history and literature, letters are important documents—an intimate look into a writer's soul, a psychological hint that illuminates a politician's decision or a philosopher's thinking, an evocation of the everyday world the letter writer inhabited. Letters convey emotions, information, points of view and serve to bind, confirm, announce, explain, revile, argue.

The fundamentals of letter writing used to be learned at home, part of the growing-up process. Letters were virtually the only way you could keep in touch with friends and relatives who lived more than a day away, so letter-writing, while art to some, was vital to all.

In our age of instant communication, in which the telephone (and now the computer) has replaced the pen, the average person devotes far less time to letter writing than ever. Most letters are now simply mailbox clutter—"junk mail" offers of every type of merchandise from records to life insurance. Computer printed, impersonal, mass produced, they have evolved from informal communicators to well-crafted sales tools. In the process, something of great value has been lost—the ability to speak directly to a single person, in a personal manner, at a leisurely, thought-provoking pace.

As a result, we now must re-teach the fundamentals of letter writing, surely one of the most important skills to be mastered in the job search process. (In fact, I think a well-crafted cover letter is *more* important than your resume.) That is the purpose of this chapter.

YOU ARE WHAT YOU WRITE

Stop for a moment and review your resume draft. It is undoubtedly (by now) a near-perfect document that instantly tells the reader the kind of job you want and why you are qualified. But does it say anything personal about you? Any amplification of your talents? Any words that are ideally "you?" Any hint of the kind of person who stands behind that resume? If you've prepared it properly, the answer should be a ringing "no"—it should be a mere sketch of your life, a bare-bones summary of your skills, education and experience.

To the general we must add the specific. That's what your letters must accomplish—adding the lines, colors and shading that will help fill out your self-portrait. This chapter will cover, in detail, the kinds of letters you will most often be called upon to prepare in your job search. There are essentially ten different types you will utilize again and again, based primarily on what each is trying to accomplish. I've included at least one well-written example of each at the end of this chapter.

ANSWER THESE QUESTIONS

Before you put pencil to paper to compose any letter, there are five key questions you must ask yourself: **Why** are you writing it? To **Whom**? **What** are you trying to accomplish?. **Which** lead will get the reader's attention? **How** do you organize the letter to best accomplish your objectives?

Why?

There should be a single, easily-definable reason you are writing any letter. This reason will often dictate what and how you write—the tone and flavor of the letter—as well as what you include or leave out.

Have you been asked in an ad to amplify your qualifications for a job, provide a salary history and portfolio samples? Then that (minimally) is your objective in writing. Limit yourself to following instructions and do a little personal selling—but very little. Including everything asked for and a simple, adequate cover letter is better than writing a "knock-'em, sock-'em" letter and omitting your salary history.

If, however, you are on a networking search, the objective of your letter is to seek out contacts who will refer you for possible informational or job interviews. In this case, getting a name and address—a referral—is your stated purpose for writing. You have to be specific and ask for this action. You will no doubt follow up with a phone call, but be certain the letter conveys what you are after. Being vague or oblique won't help you. You are after a definite yes or no when it comes to contact assistance. The recipient of your letter should know this. As they say in the world of selling, at some point you have to ask for the order.

Who?

Using the proper "tone" in a letter is as important as the content—you wouldn't write to the owner of the local meat market using the same words and style as you would employ in a letter to the director of personnel of a major company. Properly addressing the person or persons you are writing to is as important as what you say to them.

Some hints to utilize: the recipient's job title and level, his or her hiring clout (if they are just a pass along conduit, save your selling for the next step up the ladder), the kind of person they are (based on your knowledge of their area of involvement). For example, it pays to sound technical with technical people—in other words, use the kinds of words and language which they use on the job. If you have had the opportunity to speak with them, it will be easy for you. If not, and you have formed some opinions as to their types then use these as the basis of the language you employ. The cardinal rule is to say it in words you think the recipient will be comfortable hearing, not in the words you might otherwise personally choose.

What?

What do you have to offer that company? What do you have to contribute to the job, process or work situation that is unique and/or of particular benefit to the recipient of your letter. For example, if you were applying for a sales position and recently ranked number one in a summer sales job, then conveying this benefit is logical and desirable. It is a factor you may have left off your resume. Even if it was listed in your skills/accomplishment section of the resume, you can underscore and call attention to it in your letter. Repetition, when it is focused, can be a good thing.

Which?

Of all the opening sentences you can compose, which will immediately get the reader's attention? If your opening sentence is dynamic, you are already fifty percent of the way to your end objective—having your entire letter read. Don't slide into it. Know the point you are trying to make and come right to it.

How?

While a good opening is essential, how do you organize your letter so that it is easy for the recipient to read in its entirety. This is a question of flow— the way the words and sentences naturally lead one to another, holding the reader's interest until he or she reaches your signature. If you have your objective clearly in mind, this task is easier than it sounds: Simply convey your message(s) in a logical sequence. End your letter by stating what the next. steps are—yours and/or the reader's).

ONE MORE TIME

Pay attention to the small things. Neatness still counts. Have your letters typed. Spend a few extra dollars and have some personal stationary printed. And most important, make certain that your correspondence goes out quickly. The general rule is to get a letter in the mail during the week in which the project comes to your attention or in which you have had some contact with the organization. I personally attempt to mail follow-up letters the same day as the contact; at worst, within 24 hours.

WHEN TO WRITE

When do you need to write a letter?

- To answer an ad
- To prospect (many companies)
- To inquire about specific openings (single company)
- To obtain a referral
- To obtain an informational interview
- To obtain a job interview
- To say "thank you"
- To accept or reject a job offer
- To withdraw from consideration for a job

In some cases, the letter will accompany your resume; in others, it will need to stand alone. Each of the above circumstance is described in the pages that follow. I have included at least one sample of each type of letter at the end of this chapter (pp. 128 - 137).

ANSWERING AN AD

Your eye catches an ad in the Positions Available Section of the Sunday paper for a Data Entry Clerk. It tells you that the position is in a large medical office and that, though some experience would be desirable, it is not required. Well, you possess *those* skills. The ad asks that you send a letter and resume to a Post Office Box. No salary is indicated, no phone number given. You decide to reply.

Your purpose in writing—the objective (why?)—is to secure a job interview. Since no person is singled out for receipt of the ad, and since it is a large company, you assume it will be screened by the Personnel department

Adopt a professional, formal tone. You are answering a "blind" ad, so you have to play it safe. In your first sentence, refer to the ad—including the place and date of publishing and the position outlined. (Chances are this company is running more than one ad on the same date and in the same paper, so you need to identify the one to which you are replying.) Tell the reader what (specifically) you have to offer that company. Include your resume, phone number and the times it is easiest to reach you. Ask for the order—tell them you'd like to have an appointment. Sample: page 128.

BLANKET PROSPECTING LETTER

In June of this year you will graduate from a four-year college with a degree in advertising and communication. You seek a position (internship or full-time employment) in a major advertising agency's Media department. You have decided to write to fifty advertising agencies, sending each a copy of your resume. You don't know which, if any, have job openings. Sample prospecting letter: page 129.

Such blanket mailings are effective given two circumstances: 1). You must have an exemplary record and a resume which reflects it, and 2). since the response rate to such mailings is very low, you must send out a goodly number of packages.

A blanket mailing doesn't mean an impersonal one.—you should *always* be writing to a specific executive. If you have a referral, send a personalized letter to that person. If not, do *not* simply mail a package to the Personnel department; identify the department head (you'll probably be able to find the name in one of the directories listed in chapter 2) and *then* send a personalized letter. And make sure you get on the phone and follow up each letter within about ten days. Don't just sit back and wait for everyone to call you. They won't.

JUST INQUIRING

The inquiry letter is a step above the blanket prospecting letter; it's a "cold-calling" device with a twist. You have earmarked a company (and a person) as a possibility in your job search based on something you have read about them. Your general research tells you that it is a good place to work. Although you are not aware of any specific openings, you know that they employ entry-level personnel with your credentials.

While ostensibly inquiring about any openings, you are really just "referring yourself" to them in order to place your resume in front of the right person. This is what I would call a "why not?" attempt at securing a job interview. Its effectiveness depends on their actually having been in the news. This, after all, is your "excuse" for writing. Sample—page 130.

NETWORKING

It's time to get out that folder marked "Contacts" and prepare a draft networking letter. The lead sentence should be very specific, referring immediately to the friend, colleague, etc. "who suggested I write you about ..." Remember: Your objective is to secure an informational interview, pave the way for a job interview and/or get referred to still other contacts. Page 131 contains a sample networking letter.

Notice that this letter does not place the recipient in a position requiring a decision; rather, the request is couched in terms of "career advice." The second paragraph informs the reader of your level of experience. Finally, the writer is specific about seeking an appointment. Note that he indicates that the next step (scheduling) is *his*.

Unless you have been specifically asked by the referring person to do so, you will probably not be including a resume with such letters. So the letter itself must highlight your credentials, enabling the reader to gauge your relative level of experience. For entry-level personnel, education, of course, will be most important.

TO OBTAIN AN INFORMATIONAL INTERVIEW

Though the objectives of this letter are similar to those of the networking letter, they are not as personal. These are "knowledge quests" on your part and the recipient will most likely not be someone you have been referred to. The idea is to convince the reader of the sincerity of your research effort. Whatever selling you do, if you do any at all, will arise as a consequence of the meeting, not beforehand. A positive response to this type of request is in itself a good step forward. It is, after all, exposure, and amazing things can develop when people in authority agree to see you. Sample: page 132.

THANK YOUS

Although it may not always seem so, manners *do* count in the job world. But what counts even more are the simple gestures that show you actually care—like writing a thank-you letter. A well-executed, timely thank-you note tells more about your personality than anything else you may have sent. It says something about the way you were brought up—whatever else your resume tells them, you are, at least, polite, courteous and thoughtful.

Thank-you letters may well become the beginning of an all-important dialogue that leads directly to a job. So be extra careful in composing them, and make certain that they are custom made for each occasion and person. The following are the primary situations in which you will be called upon to write some variation of thank-you letter:

1). After a job interview (page 134)

2). After an informational interview (page 133)

3). Accepting a job offer (see page 135)

4). Responding to rejection: While optional, such a letter is appropriate if you have been among the finalists in a job search or were rejected due to limited experience. Remember: Some day you'll *have* enough experience; make the interviewer want to stay in touch. See page 137.

5). Withdrawing from consideration: Used when you decide you are no longer interested in a particular position. (A variation is usable for declining an actual job offer.) Whatever the reason for writing such a letter, it's wise to do so and thus keep future lines of communication open. See page 136.

SOME FINAL WORDS ABOUT STYLE

You may be wondering why so much emphasis in this book is placed on the process of letter writing. The answer lies in what might be called the area of the human dimensions. Your resume, will state the facts—unembellished, brief, to the point, it is an advertisement for yourself. The letter can fulfill an entirely different function—it is an argument for yourself, your opportunity to be creative, to convince the recipient that there is a thinking, emoting human being behind the dry credentials.

Your resume is a product of research. Your letters should be a product of thoughts, emotion and imagination. There are few hard and fast rules (except neatness), despite the sample letters I've included. Try not to make your letters overly long—a page will suffice—but imprint them with your own distinct style. Let them be you.

IN RESPONSE TO AN AD

10 E. 89th Street
New York, N.Y. 10028
December 3, 1987

The New York Times
P.O. Box 7520
New York, N.Y. 10128

Dear Sir or Madam:

This letter is in response to your advertisement for a Data Entry Clerk which appeared in the December 2nd issue of the New York Times.

I have the qualifications you are seeking. I graduated from Emerson Junior College with a degree in Word Processing. My major courses included word processing administration, office simulation and electronic keyboarding.

In addition, I have worked as a part-time laboratory assistant at Barnabus Hospital for the past two semesters. This position has provided me with hands-on experience in the medical field as well as inter-personal skills. My resume is enclosed.

I would like to have the opportunity to meet with you personally to discuss your requirements for the position. I can be reached at (212) 785-1225 between 8:00 a.m. and 5:00 p.m. and at (212) 785-4221 after 5:00 p.m. I look forward to hearing from you.

Sincerely,

Andrea Weber

Enclosure: Resume

PROSPECTING LETTER

Kim Kerr
8 Robutuck Hwy.
Hammond, IN 54054
555-875-2392

June 14, 1987

Mr. Fred Jones
Vice President - Media
Alcott & Alcott
One Lakeshore Drive
Chicago, Illinois

Dear Mr. Jones:

The name of Alcott & Alcott continually pops up in our classroom discussions of outstanding advertising agencies. Given my interest in advertising as a career and media as a specialty, I've taken the liberty of enclosing my resume.

As you can see, I have just completed a very comprehensive four years of study which included:

- o media planning
- o media research
- o demographic targeting
- o broadcast buying
- o plans evaluation

My review of the business press, especially <u>Advertising Age</u> and <u>Marketing & Media Decisions</u>, suggests that advertising will continue to play a vital role in our nation's economy and grow as our society continues to emphasize consumption of both goods and services. Though my resume does not indicate, I will be graduating in the top 10% of my class, with honors.

I will be in the Chicago area on June 29 and will call your office to see when it is convenient to arrange an appointment.

Sincerely yours,

Kim Kerr

INQUIRY LETTER

42 7th Street
Ski City, Vermont 85722
September 30, 1987

Ms. Sandra Clarkson
President
Recruitment Associates
521 West Elm Street
New Canaan, CT   23230

Dear Ms. Clarkson:

I just completed reading the article in <u>Fortune</u> on Recruitment Associates. Your innovative approach to recruiting minorities is of particular interest to me because of my background in public relations and minority recruitment.

I am interested in learning more about your work as well as the possibilities of joining your firm. My qualifications include:

- B.A. in English
- Research on minority recruitment and medical education
- Benefits Seminar participation (Univ. of Virginia)
- Reports preparation on creative writing, education and minorities

I will be in Connecticut during the week of October 10 and hope your schedule would permit us to meet briefly to discuss our mutual interests. I will call your office next week to see if such a meeting can be arranged.

I appreciate your consideration.

Sincerely yours,

Michael R. Truit

NETWORKING LETTER

Richard A. Start
42 Bach St.,
Musical City, IN 20202
317-555-1515

May 14, 1988

Ms. Michelle Fleming
Vice President
Engineering Design Associates
42 Jenkins Avenue
Fulton, Mississippi 23232

Dear Ms. Fleming:

Sam Kinnison suggested I write you. I am interested in an
entry-level design position with a firm specializing in
office construction. Sam felt it would be mutually beneficial
for us to meet and talk.

I have been educated and trained as a draftsman and have just
over two years' part-time experience in construction, design
and plans development. I am particularly interested in the
construction and design of the kinds of office projects for
which your firm is so well known.

John mentioned you as one of the leading experts in this
growing field. As I begin my job search during the next few
months, I am certain your advice would help me. Would it be
possible for us to meet briefly? My resume is enclosed.

I will call your office next week to see when your schedule
would permit such a meeting.

Sincerely,

Richard A. Start

TO OBTAIN AN INFORMATIONAL INTERVIEW

16 NW 128th Street
Raleigh, North Carolina 75755
December 2, 1988

Mr. Johnson B. McClure
Vice President - Sales
McClure Publishing
484 Smithers Road
Awkmont, North Carolina 76857

Dear Mr. McClure:

I'm sure a good deal of the credit for your company's 23% jump in space sales last year is attributable to the highly-motivated sales staff you have recruited during the last three years. I hope to work in such a position for a company just as committed to growth.

I have four years of sterling sales results to boast of, experience acquired while working my way through college. I believe my familiarity with media, sales experience and Bachelor's degree in communication from American University have properly prepared me for a career in magazine space sales.

As I begin my job search, I am trying to gather as much information and advice as possible before applying for positions. Could I take a few minutes of your time next week to discuss my career plans? I will call your office on Monday, December 12, to see if such a meeting can be arranged.

I appreciate your consideration and look forward to meeting you.

Sincerely,

Tamara S. Tepper

AFTER AN INFORMATIONAL INTERVIEW

LAZELLE WRIGHT
921 West Fourth Street
Steamboat, Colorado 72105
303-303-3030

May 21, 1988

Mr. James R. Payne
Marketing Manager
Dutton & Dutton
241 Snowridge
Ogden, Utah 72108

Dear Mr. Payne:

Jinny Clauswitz was right when she said you would be most
helpful in advising me on a career in marketing.

I appreciated your taking the time from your busy schedule to
meet with me. Your advice was most helpful and I have incor-
porated your suggestions into my resume. I will send you a copy
next week.

Again, thanks so much for your assistance. As you suggested, I
will contact Joe Simmons at Datatek next week in regards to a
possible opening with his company.

Sincerely,

Lazelle Wright

AFTER A JOB INTERVIEW

1497 Lilac Street
Old Adams, MA 01281
October 5, 1987

Mr. Rudy Delacort
Director of Personnel
First Boston Savings & Loan
175 Boylston Avenue
Boston, Massachusetts 02857

Dear Mr. Delacort:

Thank you for the opportunity to interview yesterday for the analyst trainee position. I enjoyed meeting you and Cliff Stoudt and learning more about First Boston.

Your organization appears to be growing in a direction which parallels my interests and career goals. The interview with you and your staff confirmed my initial positive impressions of First Boston, and I want to reiterate my strong interest in working for you. My prior experience as treasurer of my class plus my Business College training in accounting and finance would enable me to progress steadily through your training program and become a productive member of your research team.

Again, thank you for your consideration. If you need any additional information from me, please feel free to call.

Yours truly,

Hugh Beaumont

ACCEPTING A JOB OFFER

1497 Lilac Street
Old Adams, MA 01281
October 5, 1987

Mr. Rudy Delacort
Director of Personnel
First Boston Savings & Loan
175 Boylston Avenue
Boston, Massachusetts 02857

Dear Mr. Delacort:

I want to thank you and Mr. Stoudt for giving me the opportunity to work for
First Boston Savings & Loan. I am very pleased to accept the position as an
analyst trainee with your Investment Unit. The position entails exactly the kind
of work I want to do, and I know that I will do a good job for you.

As we discussed, I shall begin work on January 1, 1988. In the interim I shall
complete all the necessary employment forms, obtain the required physical
examination and locate housing. I plan to be in Boston within the next two
weeks and would like to deliver the paperwork to you personally. At that time,
we could handle any remaining items pertaining to my employment. I'll call
next week to schedule an appointment with you.

Sincerely yours,

Edward J. Haskell

cc: Mr. Cliff Stoudt
    Investment Unit

WITHDRAWING FROM CONSIDERATION

                                                    1497 Lilac Street
                                                    Old Adams, MA 01281
                                                    October 5, 1987

Mr. Rudy Delacort
Director of Personnel
First Boston Savings & Loan
175 Boylston Avenue
Boston, Massachusetts 02857

Dear Mr. Delacort:

It was indeed a pleasure meeting with you and Mr. Stoudt last
week to discuss your needs for an analyst trainee. Our time
together was most enjoyable and informative.

As I discussed with you during our meetings, I believe one
purpose of preliminary interviews is to explore areas of mutual
interest and to assess the fit between the individual and the
position. After careful consideration, I have decided to
withdraw from consideration for the position.

My decision is based upon two factors. First, the emphasis on
data entry is certainly needed in your case, but I would prefer
more balance in my work activities. Second, the position would
require more travel than I am willing to accept with my other
responsibilities. As I indicated, I have recently married.

I want to thank you for interviewing me and giving me the
opportunity to learn about your needs. You have a fine staff and
and I would have enjoyed working with them.

Best wishes in your search.

Yours truly,

Barbara Billingsly

cc: Mr. Cliff Stoudt
    Investment Unit

IN RESPONSE TO REJECTION

1497 Lilac Street
Old Adams, MA 01281
October 5, 1987

Mr. Rudy Delacort
Director of Personnel
First Boston Savings & Loan
175 Boylston Avenue
Boston, Massachusetts 02857

Dear Mr. Delacort:

Thank you for giving me the opportunity to interview for the analyst trainee position. I appreciate your consideration and interest in me.

Although I am disappointed in not being selected for your current vacancy, I want you to know that I appreciated the courtesy and professionalism shown to me during the entire selection process. I enjoyed meeting you, Cliff Stoudt, and the other members of your research staff. My meetings confirmed that First Boston would be an exciting place to work and build a career.

I want to reiterate my strong interest in working for you. Please keep me in mind if a similar position becomes available in the near future.

Again, thank you for the opportunity to interview and best wishes to you and your staff.

Sincerely yours,

Anthony Dow

cc: Mr. Cliff Stoudt
    Investment Unit

CHAPTER NINE

No More Sweaty Palms

You've done days of research, compiled a professional-looking and -sounding resume, contacted everyone you've known since kindergarten and written brilliant letters to the handful of companies your research has revealed are perfect matches for your own strengths, interests and abilities. Unfortunately, all of this preparatory work will be meaningless if you are unable to successfully convince one of those firms to hire you.

If you were able set up an initial meeting at one of these companies, your resume and cover letter obviously peaked *someone's* interest. Now you have to traverse the last minefield—the job interview itself. It's time to make all that preparation pay off.

This chapter will attempt to put the interview process in perspective, giving you the "inside dope" on what to expect and how to handle the questions and circumstances that arise during the course of a normal interview...and even many of those that surface in the bizarre interview situations we have all sometimes experienced.

YOUR CHANCE TO SUCCEED

Interviews shouldn't scare you. After all, the very concept of two (or more) persons meeting to determine if they are right for each other is a good one. As important as research, resumes, letters and phone calls are, they are inherently impersonal. The interview is your chance to really see and feel the company firsthand—"up close and personal;" so think of it as a positive opportunity—your chance to succeed.

That said, many of you will still be put off by the inherently inquisitive nature of the process. Though many questions *will* be asked, interviews are essentially experiments in chemistry. Are you right for the company? Is the company right for you? Not just on paper—*in the flesh*. If you decide the company *is* right for you, *your* purpose is simple and clear-cut—to convince the interviewer that you are the right person for the job; that you will fit in; and that you will be an asset to the company now and in the future. The interviewer's purpose is equally simple—to decide whether he or she should buy what you're selling.

This chapter will focus on the kinds of questions you are likely to be asked, how to answer them and the questions you should be ready to ask yourself. By removing the workings of the interview process from the "unknown" category, you will reduce the fear it engenders.

But all the preparation in the world won't completely eliminate your sweaty palms, unless you can convince yourself that the interview is an important, positive life experience from which you will benefit...even if you don't get the job. Approach it with a little enthusiasm, calm yourself and let your personality do the rest. You will undoubtedly spend an interesting hour, one that will teach you more about yourself. It's just another step in the learning process you've undertaken.

GETTING READY TO INTERVIEW

Start by setting up a calendar on which you can enter and track all your scheduled appointments. When you schedule an interview with a company, ask them how much time you should allow for the appointment. Some require all new applicants to fill out numerous forms and/or complete a battery of intelligence or psychological tests—all before the first interview. If you've only allowed an hour for the interview—and scheduled another at a nearby firm ten minutes later—the first time you confront a three-hour test series will effectively destroy any schedule.

Some companies, especially if the first interview is very positive, like to keep applicants around to talk to other executives. This process may be planned or, in a lot of cases, a spontaneous decision by an interviewer who likes you and wants you to meet some other key decision makers. Other companies will tend to schedule such a series of second interviews on a separate day. Find out, if you can, how the company you're planning to visit generally operates. Otherwise, especially if you've traveled to New York or another city to interview with a number of firms in a short period of time, a schedule that's too tight will fall apart in no time at all.

If you need to travel out-of-state to interview with a company, be sure to ask if they will be paying some or all of your travel expenses. (It's generally expected that you'll be paying your own way to firms within your home state.) If they don't offer—and you don't ask—presume you're paying the freight.

Even if the company agrees to reimburse you, make sure you have enough money to pay all the expenses yourself. While some may reimburse you immediately, handing you a check as you leave the building, the majority of firms may take from a week to a month to forward you an expense check.

PRE-INTERVIEW RESEARCH

The research you did to find these companies is nothing compared to the research you need to do now that you're beginning to narrow your search. If you followed our detailed suggestions when you started targeting these firms in the first place, you've already amassed a lot of information about them. If you didn't do the research *then*, you sure better decide to do it *now*. Study each company as if you were going to be tested on your detailed knowledge of their organization and operations. Here's a complete checklist of the facts you should try to know about each company you plan to visit for a job interview:

The Basics

1. The address of (and directions to) the office you're visiting
2. Headquarters location (if different)
3. Some idea of domestic and international branches
4. Relative size (compared to other companies)
5. Annual billings, sales) and/or income (last two years)
6. Subsidiary companies; specialized divisions
7. Departments (overall structure)
8. Major accounts, products or services

The Subtleties

1. History of the firm (specialties, honors, awards, famous names, etc.)
2. Names, titles and backgrounds of top management
3. Existence (and type) of training program
4. Relocation policy
5. Relative salaries (compared to other companies in field or by size)
6. Recent developments concerning the the company and its products or services (from your trade magazine and newspaper reading)
7. Everything you can learn about the career, likes and dislikes of the person(s) interviewing you

The amount of time and work necessary to be *this* well prepared for an interview is considerable. It will not be accomplished the day before the interview. You may even find some of the information you need to be unavailable on short notice. (Is it really so important to do all this? Well, *some*body out there is going to. And if you happen to be interviewing for the same job as that other, well-prepared, knowledgeable candidate, who do *you* think will impress the interviewer more?)

As we've already discussed, if you give yourself enough time, most of this information is surprisingly easy to obtain. In addition to the reference sources we covered in chapter 2, the company itself can probably supply you with a great deal of data. A firm's Annual Report—which all publicly-owned companies must publish yearly for their stockholders—is a virtual treasure trove of information. Write each company and request copies of their last two Annual Reports. A comparison of sales, income and other data over this period may enable you to infer some interesting things about their overall financial health and growth potential. Many libraries also have collections of annual reports from major corporations.

Attempting to learn about your interviewer is a chore, the importance of which is underestimated by most applicants (who then, of course, don't bother to do it). Being one of the exceptions may get you a job. Use the biographical references covered in chapter 2. If he or she is listed in any of these sources, you'll be able to learn an awful lot about his or her background. In addition, find out if he or she has written any articles that have appeared in the trade press or, even better, books on his or her area(s) of expertise. Referring to these writings during the course of an interview, without making it *too* obvious a compliment, can be very effective. We all have egos and we all like people to talk about us. The interviewer is no different from the rest of us. You might also check to see if any of your networking contacts worked with him or her at his current (or a previous) company and can help "fill you in."

SCREENING VS. SELECTION INTERVIEWS

The process to which the majority of this chapter is devoted is the actual *selection interview,* usually conducted by the person to whom the new hire will be reporting. But there is another process—the *screening interview*—which many of you may have to survive first.

Screening interviews are usually conducted by a member of the Personnel department. Though they may not be empowered to hire, these people *are* in a position to screen out or eliminate those candidates they feel (based on the facts) are not qualified to handle the job. These decisions are not usually made on the basis of personality, appearance, eloquence, persuasiveness or any other subjective criteria, but rather by clicking off yes or no answers against a checklist of skills. If you don't have the requisite number, you will be eliminated from further consideration. This may seem arbitrary, but it is a realistic and often necessary way for corporations to minimize the time and dollars involved in filling even the lowest jobs on the corporate ladder.

Remember, screening personnel are not looking for reasons to *hire* you; they're trying to find ways to *eliminate* you. Resumes sent blindly to the Personnel department will usually be subjected to such screening; you'll be eliminated without any personal contact (a good reason to put together a superior resume and *not* send out blind mailings).

If you are contacted, it will most likely be by telephone. When you are responding to such a call, keep these three things in mind: 1). It *is* an interview; be on your guard. 2). Answer all questions honestly. And 3). Be enthusiastic. You will get the standard questions from the interviewer—his or her attempts to "flesh out" the information included on your resume and/or cover letter. Strictly speaking, they are seeking out any negatives which may exist. If your resume is honest and factual (and it should be), you have no reason to be anxious, because you have nothing to hide.

Don't be nervous—be glad you were called and remember your objective: to get past this screening phase so you can get on to the real interview.

THE DAY OF THE INTERVIEW

On the day of the interview, wear a conservative (not funereal) business suit—not a sports coat, not a "nice" blouse and skirt. Shoes should be shined, nails cleaned, hair cut and in place. And ladies: no low-cut or tight-fitting dresses.

It's not unusual for resumes and cover letters to head in different directions when a company starts passing them around to a number of executives. If you sent them, both may even be long gone. So bring along extra copies of your resume and your own copy of the cover letter that originally accompanied it. Whether or not you make them available, we suggest you prepare a neatly-typed list of references (including the name, title, company, address and phone number of each person). You may want to bring along a copy of your high school or college transcript, especially if it's something to brag about. (Once you get your first job, you'll probably never use it—or be asked for it—again, so enjoy it while you can!) And, if appropriate or required, make sure you bring samples of your work (e.g., clippings, portfolio, etc.).

On Time Means Fifteen Minutes Early

Plan to arrive fifteen minutes before your scheduled appointment. If you're in an unfamiliar city or have a long drive to their offices, allow extra time for the unexpected delays that seem to occur with mind-numbing regularity on important days.

Arriving early will give you some time to check your appearance, catch your breath, check in with the receptionist, learn how to correctly pronounce the interviewer's name and get yourself organized and battle ready.

Arriving late does not make a sterling first impression. If you are only a few minutes late, it's probably best not to mention it or even excuse yourself. With a little luck, everybody else is behind schedule and no one will notice. However, if you're more than fifteen minutes late, have an honest (or at least *serviceable)* explanation ready and offer it at your first opportunity. Then drop the subject as quickly as possible and move on to the interview.

The Eyes Have It

When you meet the interviewer, shake hands firmly. People pay attention to handshakes. Ask for a business card. This will make sure you get the name and title right when you write your follow-up letter. You can staple it to the company file for easy reference as you continue your networking.

Try to maintain eye contact with the interviewer as you talk. This will indicate you're interested in what he or she has to say. Sit straight. Avoid smoking. Should coffee or a soft drink be offered, you may accept (but should do so only if the interviewer is joining you). Keep your voice at a comfortable level, and try to sound enthusiastic (without imitating a cheerleader). Be confident and poised, and provide direct, accurate and honest answers to the trickiest questions. And, as you try to remember all this, just be yourself, and try to act like you're comfortable and almost enjoying yourself!

Don't Name Drop

A friendly relationship with other company employees may have provided you with valuable information prior to the interview, but don't flaunt such relationships. The interviewer is interested only in how you will relate to him or her and how well he or she surmises you will fit in with the rest of the staff. Name dropping may smack of favoritism. And you are in no position to know who the interviewer's favorite (and *least* favorite) people are.

Fork On The Left, Knife On The Right

Interviews are sometimes conducted over lunch, though this is not usually the case with entry-level people. If it does happen to you, though, try to order something in the middle price range, neither filet mignon nor a cheeseburger. Do not order alcohol. If your interviewer orders a carafe of wine, you may share it. Otherwise, alcohol should be considered *verboten*, under any and all circumstances. Then hope your mother taught you the correct way to eat and talk at the same time. If not, just do your best to maintain your poise.

Last Impressions May Be The First Remembered

There are some things interviewers will always view with displeasure—street language, complete lack of eye contact, insufficient or vague explanations or answers, a noticeable lack of energy, poor interpersonal skills (i.e., not listening or the basic inability to carry on an intelligent conversation), and a demonstrable lack of motivation.

Small oversights can cost you a job. Phil Mushnick, a regular sports columnist for the *New York Post*, describes the seemingly insignificant incident that, legend has it, made Joe Namath the quarterback for the New York Jets football team:

>"If not for one rainy night in 1964, Namath might never have become a Jet. On that evening, (Jets' owner) Sonny and Mrs. Werblin were entertaining Tulsa University quarterback Jerry Rhome at a Manhattan restaurant. Werblin was also entertaining plans to draft Rhome and build the franchise around him, much the way he would with Namath.

>"Legend has it that, following dinner, Rhome made a solo dash for Werblin's car, which was waiting outside in the rain, leaving the Werblins to soak while he climbed in first. Friends of Werblin say that episode convinced him that Rhome wasn't the (quarterback) he wanted to lead his team. Shortly afterwards, the Jets traded Rhome's draft rights to Houston for a No. 1 pick, which they used to select Namath."

As the above story demonstrates, even if it's more legend than fact, every impression may count. And the very *last* impression an interviewer has may outweigh everything else. So, before you allow an interview to end, summarize why you want the job, why you are qualified, and what, in particular, you can offer their company.

Then, take some action. If the interviewer hasn't told you about the rest of the interview process and/or where you stand, ask him or her. Will you be seeing other people that day? If so, ask for some background on the other people with whom you'll be interviewing. If there are no other meetings that day, what's the next step? When can you expect to hear from them about coming back?

When you return home, file all the business cards, copies of correspondence and notes from the interview(s) with each company in the appropriate files. Finally, but most importantly, ask yourself which firms you really want to work for and which you are no longer interested in. This will quickly determine how far you want the process at each to develop before you politely tell them to stop considering you for the job.

Immediately send a thank-you letter to each executive you met. These should, of course, be neatly-typed business letters, not handwritten notes (unless you are most friendly, indeed, with the interviewer and want to *stress* the "informal" nature of your note). If you are still interested in pursuing a position at their company, tell them in no uncertain terms. Reiterate why you feel you're the best candidate and tell each of the executives when you hope (expect?) to hear from them.

NOT ALL INTERVIEWERS ARE CREATED EQUAL

Though most interviews will follow a relatively standard format, there will undoubtedly be a wide disparity in the interviewing skills of the interviewers you meet. Many of these executives (with the exception of the Personnel staff) will most likely not have extensive interviewing experience, have limited knowledge of interviewing techniques, use them infrequently, be hurried or harried by the press of other duties or not even view your interview as critically important.

Rather than studying standardized test results or utilizing professional evaluation skills developed over many years of practice, these nonprofessionals react intuitively—their initial (first five minutes) impressions are often the lasting and overriding factors they remember. So you must sell yourself ...fast.

The best way to do this is to try to achieve a comfort level with your interviewer. Isn't establishing rapport—through words, gestures, appearance common interests, etc.—what you try to do in *any* social situation? It's just trying to know one another better. Against this backdrop, the questions and answers will flow in a more natural way.

THE SET SEQUENCE

Irrespective of the competence levels of the interviewer, you can anticipate an interview sequence roughly as follows:

- Greetings
- Social niceties (small talk)
- Purpose of meeting (let's get down to business)
- Broad questions/answers
- Specific questions/ answers
- In-depth discussion of company, job and opportunity
- Summarizing information given & received
- Possible salary probe (dependent upon level of achievement)
- Summary/indication as to next steps

When you look at this sequence closely, it is obvious that once you have gotten past the greeting, social niceties and some explanation of the job (in the "getting down to business" section), the bulk of the interview will be questions—yours and the interviewer's. In this question and answer session, there are not necessarily any right or wrong answers, only good and bad ones.

IT'S TIME TO PLAY Q & A

You can't control the "chemistry" between you and the interviewer—do you seem to "hit it off" right from the start or never connect at all? Since you *can't* control such a subjective problem, it pays to focus on what you *can* —the questions you will be asked, your answers and the questions *you* should ask.

Not surprisingly, many of the same questions pop up in interview after interview, regardless of company size, type or location. We have chosen the thirteen most common—along with appropriate hints and answers for each—for inclusion in this chapter. Remember: There are no right or wrong answers to these questions, only good and bad ones.

Substance counts more than speed when answering questions. Take your time and make sure that you listen to each question—there is nothing quite as disquieting as a lengthy, well-thought-out answer that is completely irrelevant to the question asked. You wind up looking like a programmed clone with stock answers to dozens of questions who has, unfortunately, pulled the wrong answer out of the grab bag.

Once you have adequately answered a specific question, it *is* permissible to go beyond it and add more information if doing so adds something to the discussion and/or highlights a particular strength, skill, course, etc. But avoid making lengthy speeches just for the sake of sounding off.

Study the list of questions (and hints) that follow, and prepare at least one solid, concise answer that you can trot out on cue. Practice with a friend until your answers to these most-asked questions sound intelligent, professional and, most important, unmemorized and unrehearsed.

"Why do you want to be in this field?"

Using your knowledge and understanding of the particular field, explain why you find the business exciting and where and how you see yourself fitting in.

"Why do you think you'll be successful in this business?"

Using the information from your self evaluation and the research you did on that particular company, formulate an answer which marries your strengths to theirs and to the characteristics of the position for which you're applying.

"Why did you choose our company?"

This is an excellent opportunity to explain the extensive process of education and research you've undertaken. Tell them about your strengths and how you match up with their firm. Emphasize specific things about their company that led you to seek an interview. Be a salesperson—be convincing.

"What can you do for us?"

Construct an answer that essentially lists your strengths, the experience you have which will contribute to your job performance, and any other unique qualifications that will place you at the head of the applicant pack. Be careful: This is a question specifically designed to *eliminate* some of that pack. Sell yourself. Be one of the few called back for a second interview.

"What position here interests you?"

If you're interviewing for a specific position, answer accordingly. If you want to make sure you don't close the door on other opportunities of which you might be unaware, you can follow up with your own question: "I'm here to apply for your Account Executive Training Program. Is there another position open for which you feel I'm qualified?"

If you've arranged an interview with a company without knowing of any specific openings, use the answer to this question to describe the kind of work you'd like to do and why you're qualified to do it. Avoid a specific job title, since they will tend to vary from firm to firm.

If you're on a first interview with the personnel department, just answer the question. They only want to figure out where to send you.

"What jobs have you held and why did you leave them?"

Or the direct approach: "Have you ever been fired?" Take the opportunity to expand on your resume, rather than precisely answering the question by merely recapping your job experiences. In discussing each job, point out what you liked about it, what factors led to your leaving and how the next job added to your continuing professional education. If you *have* been fired, say so. It's very easy to check.

"What are your strengths and weaknesses?" or "What are your hobbies (or outside interests)?"

Both questions can be easily answered using the data you gathered to complete the self-evaluation process. Be wary of being too forthcoming about your glaring faults (nobody expects you to volunteer every weakness and mistake), but do *not* reply, "I don't have any." They won't believe you and, what's worse, *you* won't believe you. After all, you did the evaluation—you know it's a lie!

Good answers to these questions are those in which the interviewer can identify benefits for him- or herself. For example: "I consider myself an excellent planner. I am seldom caught by surprise and I prize myself on being able to anticipate problems and schedule my time to be ahead of the game. I devote a prescribed number of hours each week to this activity. I've noticed that many people just react. If you plan ahead, you should be able to cut off most problems before they arise."

You may consider disarming the interviewer by admitting a weakness, but doing it in such a way as to make it relatively unimportant to the job function. For example: "Higher mathematics has never been my strong suit. Though I am competent enough, I've always envied my friends with a more mathematical bent. In sales, though, I haven't found this a liability. I'm certainly quick enough in figuring out how close I am to monthly quotas and, of course, I keep a running record of commissions earned."

"Do you think your extracurricular activities were worth the time you devoted to them?"

This is a question often asked of entry-level candidates. One possible answer: "Very definitely. As you see I have been quite active in the Student Government and French Club. My language fluency allowed me to spend my junior year abroad as an exchange student, and working in a functioning government gave me firsthand knowledge of what can be accomplished with people in the real world. I suspect my marks would have been somewhat higher had I not taken on so much, but I feel the balance it gave me contributed significantly to my overall growth as a person."

"What are your career goals?"

Interviewers are always seeking to probe the motivations of prospective employees. Nowhere is this more apparent than when the area of ambition is discussed. The high key answer to this question might be; "Given hard work, company growth and a few lucky breaks along the way, I'd look forward to being in a top executive position by the time I'm 35. I believe in effort and the risk/reward system—my research on this company has shown me that it operates on the same principles. I would hope it would select its future leaders from those people who displaying such characteristics."

"At some future date would you be willing to relocate?"

Pulling up one's roots is not the easiest thing in the world to do, but it is often a fact of life in the corporate world. If you're serious about your career (and such a move often represents a step up the career ladder), you will probably not mind such a move. Tell the interviewer. If you really *don't* want to move, you may want to say so, too—though I would find out how probable or frequent such relocations would be before closing the door while still in the interview stage.

"How would you describe your relationship with your last supervisor?"

This question is designed to understand your relationship with (and reaction to) authority. Remember: Companies look for team players, people who will fit in with their hierarchy, their rules, their ways of doing things. An answer might be: "I prefer to work with smart, strong people who know what they want and can express themselves. I learned in the military that in order to accomplish the mission, someone has to be the leader and that person has to be given the authority to lead. Someday I aim to be that leader. I hope then my subordinates will follow me as much and as competently as I'm ready to follow now."

"What are your salary requirements?"

If they are at all interested in you, this question will probably come up. The danger, of course, is that you may price yourself too low or, even worse, right out of a job you want. Since you will have a general idea of industry figures for that position (and may even have an idea of what that company tends to pay new people for the position), why not refer to a *range* of salaries, such as "$16,000 - $19,000?"

If the interviewer doesn't bring up salary at all, it's doubtful you're being seriously considered, so you probably don't need to even bring the subject up. (If you know you aren't getting the job or aren't interested in it if offered, you may try to nail down a salary figure in order to be better prepared for the next interview.)

"Tell me about yourself."

Watch out for this one! It's often one of the first questions asked. If you falter here, the rest of the interview could quickly become a downward slide to nowhere. Be prepared, and consider it an opportunity to combine your answers to many of the previous questions into one concise description of who you are, what you want to be and why that company should take a chance on you. Summarize your resume—briefly—and expand on particular courses or experiences relevant to the firm or position. Do not go on about your hobbies or personal life, your dog, where you spent your summer vacation, etc. None of that is particularly relevant to securing that job. You may explain how that particular job fits in with your long-range career goals and talk specifically about what attracted you to their company in the first place.

THE NOT-SO-OBVIOUS QUESTIONS

Every interviewer is different and, unfortunately, there are no rules saying he or she has to use all or any of the "basic" questions covered above. But we think the odds are against his or her avoiding *all* of them. Whichever of these he or she includes, be assured most interviewers do like to come up with questions that are "uniquely theirs." It may be just one or a whole series— questions developed over the years that he or she feels help separate the wheat from the chaff.

You can't exactly prepare yourself for questions like, "What would you do if...(fill in the blank with some obscure occurrence)?," "Tell me about your father," or "What's your favorite ice cream flavor?" Every interviewer we know has his or her favorites and all of these questions seem to come out of left field. Just stay relaxed, grit your teeth (quietly) and take a few seconds to frame a reasonably intelligent reply.

Some questions may be downright inappropriate. Young women, for example, may be asked about their plans for marriage and children. Don't call the interviewer a chauvinist (or worse). And don't point out that the ques-tion may be a little outside the law. (The nonprofessional interviewer may not realize such questions are illegal, and a huffy response may confuse—even anger—him or her.) Whenever any questions are raised about your personal life—and this question surely qualifies—it is much more effective to respond that you are very interested in the position and have no reason to believe that your personal life will preclude you from doing an excellent job.

"DO YOU HAVE ANY QUESTIONS?"

It's the last fatal question on our list—often the last one an interviewer throws at you—after an hour or two of grilling. Unless the interview has been very long and unusually thorough, you probably *should* have questions about the job, the company, or even the industry. Unfor-tunately, by the time this question off-handedly hits the floor, you are already looking forward to leaving and may have absolutely nothing to say.

Preparing yourself for an interview means more than having answers for some of the questions an interviewer may ask. It means having your *own* set of questions—at least five or six—for the interviewer. The interviewer is trying to find the right person for the job. *You*'re trying to find the right job. So you should be just as curious about him or her and the company as he or she is about you. Here's a short list of questions you may consider asking on any interview:

1. What will my typical day be like?

2. What happened to the last person who had this job?

3. Given my attitude and qualifications, how would you estimate my chances for career advancement at your company?

4. Why did you come to work here? What keeps you here?

5. If you were I, would you start here again?

6. How would you characterize the management philosophy of your firm?

7. What characteristics do the successful_____ at your company have in common (fill in the blank with an appropriate title, such as "writers," "accountants," "salespeople," etc.)?

8. What's the best (and worst) thing about working here?

9. On a scale of 1 to 10, how would you rate your company—in terms of salaries, benefits and employee satisfaction—in comparison to other firms your size?

Other questions about the company or position will be obvious—they're the areas your research hasn't been able to fill in. Ask the interviewer. But be careful and use common sense. No one is going to answer highly personal, rude or indiscreet questions. Even innocent questions might be misconstrued if you don't think about the best way to pose them—*before* they come trippingly off your tongue.

TESTING & APPLICATIONS

Though not part of the selection interview itself, job applications and psychological testing are often part of the pre-interview process. You should know something about them.

The job application is essentially a record-keeping exercise—simply the transfer of work experience and educational data from your resume to a printed applications form.Though taking the time to simply recopy data may seem like a waste of time, some companies simply want the information in a particular order on a standard form. One difference: Applications often require the listing of references and salary levels achieved. Be sure to bring your list of references with you to any interview (so you can transfer the pertinent information) and don't lie about salary history; it's easily checked.

Many companies now use a variety of psychological tests as additional mechanisms to screen out undesirable candidates. Although their accuracy is subject to question, the companies that use them obviously believe they are effective at identifying applicants whose personality makeups would preclude their participating positively in a given work situation, especially those at the extreme ends of the behavior spectrum. Essentially, they will get a reading on the extremes of behavior.

Their usefulness in predicting job accomplishment is considered limited. If you are normal (like the rest of us), you'll have no trouble with these tests and may even find them amusing. Just don't try to outsmart them— you'll just wind up outsmarting yourself.

STAND UP AND BE COUNTED:

Your interview is over. Breathe a sigh of relief. Make your notes—you'll want to keep a file on the important things covered and for use in your next interview. Some people consider one out of ten (one job offer for every ten interviews) a good score...if you're keeping score. We suggest you don't. It's virtually impossible to judge how others are judging you. Just go on to the next interview. Sooner than you think, you'll be hired. For the right job.

Index

Q

R

S

T

U

V

W

X, Y, Z

MAIL ORDER COUPON

Name: _____

Mailing Address: _____

City, State, Zip Code: _____

Telephone:_____ ❑ **CHECK HERE FOR CATALOG**

Quantity	Binding	Title	Price
SERIES TITLES (Add postage and handling)			
_____	Paper	Internships, Vol 1.	$11.95
_____	Paper	Internships, Vol. 2	$11.95
_____	Paper	Advertising Career Directory	$26.95
_____	Paper	Book Publishing Career Directory	$26.95
_____	Paper	Magazines Career Directory	$26.95
_____	Paper	Marketing & Sales Career Directory	$26.95
_____	Paper	Newspapers Career Directory	$26.95
_____	Paper	Public Relations Career Directory	$26.95
_____	Hardcover	Advertising Career Directory	$34.95
_____	Hardcover	Book Publishing Career Directory	$34.95
_____	Hardcover	Magazines Career Directory	$34.95
_____	Hardcover	Marketing & Sales Career Directory	$34.95
_____	Hardcover	Newspapers Career Directory	$34.95
_____	Hardcover	Public Relations Career Directory	$34.95
NON-SERIES TITLES (Prices include postage and handling)			
_____	Paper	College Comes Sooner Than You Think!	$11.95
_____	Paper	Your First Resume Book	$11.95
_____	Paper	High Impact Resumes & Letters	$13.95
_____	Paper	Interview for Success	$11.95
_____	Paper	Complete Guide to Public Employment	$15.50
_____	Paper	Public Schools USA	$14.95
_____	Paper	International Careers: An Insider's Guide	$11.95
_____	Paper	After College: The Business of Getting Jobs	$11.95
_____	Paper	Parenting Through the College Years	$11.95
_____	Paper	What's Next? Career Strategies After 35	$11.95
_____	Paper	Complete Guide to Social Security	$11.95

Total number of Series volumes ordered: _____ Amount : $_____

$2.50 per order plus $1.00 per volume shipping charges $_____

Total number of non-Series volumes: _____ Amount: $_____

Total amount of order. <u>This must be enclosed.</u> $_____

NON-SERIES TITLES

- ❑ **COLLEGE COMES SOONER THAN YOU THINK! The College Planning Guide For High School Students And Their Families,** by Jill Reilly and Bonnie Featherstone. ISBN 0-934829-24-1, Paper, 6 x 9, 176 pp. $11.95 postpaid.

- ❑ **YOUR FIRST RESUME: The Comprehensive Preparation Guide for High School and College Students** by Ronald W. Fry. ISBN 0-934829-25-X, Paper, 8 1/2 x 11, 160 pp. (approx.). $11.95 postpaid.

- ❑ **HIGH IMPACT RESUMES AND LETTERS: How to Communicate Your Qualifications to Employers,** 3rd Edition, by Dr. Ronald L. Krannich and William J. Banis. ISBN 0-942710-20-7, Paper, 8 1/2 x 11, 180 pages. $13.95

- ❑ **INTERVIEW FOR SUCCESS: A Practical Guide To Increasing Job Interviews, Offers and Salaries,** by Drs. Caryl & Ron Krannich. ISBN 0-942710-19-3, Paper, 6 x 9, Indexed & Illustrated, 165 pages. $11.95 postpaid.

- ❑ **THE COMPLETE GUIDE TO PUBLIC EMPLOYMENT,** by Drs. Ron and Caryl Krannich. ISBN 0-942710-05-3, Paper, 6 x 9, 512 pages. $15.50 postpaid.

- ❑ **PUBLIC SCHOOLS USA: A Guide To School Districts,** by Charles Harrison ISBN 0-913589-36-5, Paper, 6 x 9, 256 pages. $14.95 postpaid.

- ❑ **INTERNATIONAL CAREERS: An Insiders Guide,** by David Rearwin. ISBN 0-913589-28-4, Paper, 6 x 9, 192 pages. $11.95 postpaid.

- ❑ **AFTER COLLEGE; The Business of Getting Jobs,** by Jack Falvey ISBN 0-913589-17-9, Paper, 6 x 9, 192 pages. $11.95 postpaid.

- ❑ **PARENTING THROUGH THE COLLEGE YEARS,** by Norman Giddan and Sally Vallongo ISBN 0-913589-37-3, Paper, 6 x 9, 192 pages. $11.95 postpaid.

- ❑ **WHAT'S NEXT?/Career Strategies After 35,** by Jack Falvey. ISBN 0-913589-26-8 Paper, 6 x 9, 192 pages. $11.95 postpaid.

- ❑ **THE COMPLETE & EASY GUIDE TO SOCIAL SECURITY AND MEDI-CARE,** by Faustin F. Jehle. ISBN 0-930045-02-5, Paper, 8 1/2 x 11, 175 pages. $11.95 postpaid.

TO ORDER ANY OF THESE TITLES—OR TO REQUEST A CATALOG—SIMPLY FILL OUT THE ORDER FORM ON THE OPPOSITE PAGE OR CALL **1-800-CAREER-1** TO USE YOUR MASTERCARD OR VISA.

GREAT BOOKS FROM THE CAREER PRESS

TO ORDER ANY OF THESE ACCLAIMED VOLUMES or request a catalog, **CALL 1-800-CAREER-1.** For your convenience, we accept MASTERCARD and VISA.

Or simply check the titles you would like on the coupon on the preceding page, fill out the required information completely, tear out the entire page and send (with full payment if you are ordering books) to: The Career Press, 62 Beverly Rd., PO Box 34, Hawthorne, N.J. 07057.

SERIES TITLES:

❑ **INTERNSHIPS, VOL. 1: ADVERTISING, MARKETING, PUBLIC RELA-TIONS & SALES,** edited by Ronald W. Fry. ISBN 0-934829-27-6, Paper, 6 x 9, 320 pages (approx.). $11.95.

❑ **INTERNSHIPS, VOL 2: NEWSPAPER, MAGAZINE AND BOOK PUBLISH-ING,** edited by Ronald W. Fry. ISBN 0-934829-28-4, Paper, 6 x 9, 320 pages (approx.). $11.95.

ADVERTISING CAREER DIRECTORY, 3rd edition, 352 pages, 8 1/2 x 11
❑ Paper — ISBN 0-934829-30-6, $26.95.
❑ Hardcover (cloth) — ISBN 0-934829-40-3, $34.95.

MARKETING & SALES CAREER DIRECTORY, 2nd edition, 384 pages, 8 1/2 X 11.
❑ Paper — ISBN 0-934829-34-9, $26.95.
❑ Hardcover (cloth) — ISBN 0-934829-44-6, $34.95.

PUBLIC RELATIONS CAREER DIRECTORY, 3rd edition, 384 PAGES, 8 1/2 X 11.
❑ Paper — ISBN 0-934829-33-0, $26.95.
❑ Hardcover (cloth) — ISBN 0-934829-43-8, $34.95.

MAGAZINES CAREER DIRECTORY, 3rd edition, 352 pages, 8 1/2 X 11.
❑ Paper — ISBN 0-934829-31-4, $26.95.
❑ Hardcover (cloth) — ISBN 0-934829-41-1, $34.95.

BOOK PUBLISHING CAREER DIRECTORY, 3rd edition, 256 pages, 8 1/2 X 11.
❑ Paper — ISBN 0-934829-32-2, $26.95.
❑ Hardcover (cloth) — ISBN 0-934829-42-X, $34.95.

NEWSPAPERS CAREER DIRECTORY, 2nd edition, 288 pages, 8 1/2 X 11.
❑ Paper — ISBN 0-934829-35-7, $26.95.
❑ Hardcover (cloth) — ISBN 0-934829-45-4, $34.95

Please enclose $2.50 per order and $1.00 per title for each series volume ordered.

* * * MORE BOOKS AND MAIL ORDER COUPON ON PRECEDING PAGES * * *